A PIECE OF THE ACTION

A PIECE OF THE
action

INTEGRATING PERSONAL AND CORPORATE GOALS

By Konosuke Matsushita

PHP INSTITUTE, INC.
TOKYO • KYOTO • NEW YORK • SINGAPORE

This book was originally published in
Japanese by PHP Institute, Inc.
under the title *Shain kokoroecho* [Precepts for
employees] and *Jinsei kokoroecho* [Precepts
for Living]. Translated by Lynne E. Riggs,
Dean Robson and Manabu Takechi.

■

Published by PHP Institute, Inc.
Tokyo Head Office:
3-10 Sanbancho, Chiyoda-ku, Tokyo 102 Japan.
Kyoto Head Office: 11 Kitanouchicho, Nishikujo,
Minami-ku, Kyoto 601 Japan.
Distributed in North America and Europe by
PHP Institute of America, Inc.
400 Madison Avenue Suite 305, New York, New York
10017 U.S.A., and in Asia and Oceania by
PHP International (S) Pte., Ltd., 20 Cecil Street
#15-07, The Quadrant, Singapore 0104,
The Republic of Singapore; and in Japan by
PHP Institute, Inc.

■

■

Printed in Japan by Tosho Printing Co., Ltd.
Cover design by Michael Gilmore and
book design and typography by Koitsu Taniguchi.
Typesetting by Asahi Media International Inc.
The main text is set in
11-point Utopia Regular. Linotronic 300.

■

First Edition, September 1993
ISBN4-569-54147-X

Contents

To the Reader

Konosuke Matsushita, the founder of both Matsushita Electric and PHP Institute started his career at the tender age of nine when he became an apprentice in a brazier shop in Osaka. For eighty-five years thereafter, until he passed away at the age of 94, he consistently stressed the importance, both as an individual and as an entrepreneur, of increasing the zest and satisfaction to be derived from one's work. He was convinced that anyone—himself, the employees of Matsushita Electric, and the public at large—who was enthusiastic about work and found it personally rewarding would also find life that much more exhilarating and satisfying. The more people that felt this way, the more the quality of life in the community would be enhanced. Enthusiasm is infectious.

In the latter part of his life he wrote two books which dealt with this subject from the corporate and the private perspective. We have translated these and put them together in this volume to give the reader a glimpse into the mind of one of the great industrialists of our age. You may not agree with all the points he makes, but you will almost certainly find ample food for thought in each of the essays.

Part One is a translation of *Shain kokoroecho* (Precepts for Employees) which was written in 1981 at the age of 86. In these chapters Konosuke Matsushita presents his thoughts on issues that may trouble employees at different stages of their journey in the corporate world.

Part Two is a translation of *Jinsei kokoroecho* (Precepts for Life) which was written in 1984 at the age of 89. Here he presents his own personal philosophy of life in the form of ruminations on a variety of topics, and offers some sage suggestions on ways to make life satisfying and enjoyable.

Dramatic developments in technology, transportation, and communications have made it possible and even fashionable to talk of living in a global village, but they have also ensured that life in that village is more frenetic than idyllic. All too often we find ourselves working at a frantic pace without any clear conception of what we are doing or why. The result is neither efficient nor satisfying. We hope that this volume of essays by Konosuke Matsushita can provide its readers with some small respite and allow them to take their bearings once again.

Lastly, I would like to express my heartfelt gratitude to Lynne E. Riggs, Dean Robson and Manabu Takechi of the Center for Intercultural Communication for their careful translation, to Patricia Murray for her skillful editing, and to Michael Gilmore for his elegant book design.

TORU YAMAGUCHI
Executive Director
PHP Institute, Inc.
August 1993

A Note About the Author

KONOSUKE MATSUSHITA'S NAME means "lucky man under the pine tree," fitting for the man who founded one of the world's top industrial corporations. Matsushita was born near Osaka in 1894 into a wealthy family, but his father's speculation on the rice market ate up the family fortune. At fifteen, he began working at the Osaka Electric Light Company, leaving when he was twenty-three to start a company to produce a socket he'd invented. Later he added an adaptor plug and bicycle lamp to his line-up; by 1925, his products successful, he began using the brand name "National."

In 1946, in response to the destruction wrought by World War II, Matsushita founded the PHP Institute to foster a peaceful society, rich both materially and spiritually. PHP stands for "peace and happiness through prosperity." He endowed the Matsushita School of Government and Management in 1980 to train potential leaders to resolve problems facing Japan and the world. He created the Japan Prize in 1983 to honor scientific and technological contributions to peace and prosperity. Until his death in 1989 at the age of ninety-four, Matsushita took equally keen interest in his global industrial empire and in humanitarian projects.

PART ONE
Setting into the Corporate World

Preface

In INDUSTRY TODAY, conditions are changing at an extremely rapid and often bewildering speed. Business know-how and technology that is at the cutting edge one day can easily become outmoded the next. And the pace of change is likely to grow even faster and more startling in the years ahead. In order to cope with this fast-moving world, people in business, managers and employees alike, have to constantly strive to improve their professional and technical skills.

The task of enhancing our abilities and improving the caliber of our work on our own initiative may seem daunting at first, but if we take up the task with a positive attitude, I believe we reap a rich harvest in the added sense of fulfillment we derive from our work as employees of a company and increased quality of our lives as human beings.

The work we do is, or should be, an endless source of exploration and experience; the longer we pursue a particular vocation, the more we understand its inner secrets and possibilities. And it is the accumulation of our own assiduous efforts on the job—of days when we can honestly congratulate ourselves for having done a good job—that help us to grow and enhance the fruits of our endeavors. If, moreover, we can also feel that, through our work and through the activities of the company we are a part of, we are doing something that is useful and helpful to others, then we will be able to savor the true satisfaction and enjoyment of being part of a corporate organization.

This volume consists of reflective essays on topics I consider important to persons working in business and industry. They are all themes I repeated to the staff and employees of Matsushita Electric throughout my business career, and they are all precepts of the most basic, ordinary, and common sense order, drawn from my experience and reflections over the years. At a time of dramatic change like today, it is more important than ever for us to grasp and firmly adhere to basic rules such as these to guide our thinking and behavior. I hope that these essays will be useful both in the efforts of people in business to enlighten and improve their professional endeavors and to help like their work to more fulfilled lives as a whole.

In addition to this collection focusing on precepts for businessmen, I have also set down my thoughts on related subjects in other publications including *Not for Bread Alone: A Business Ethos, A Management Ethic,* and *My Management Philosophy* and *Velvet Glove, Iron Fist: And Other Dimensions of Leadership.* I hope that they may be used as tools for the cultivation and encouragement of a sensitive and capable work force.

Konosuke Matsushita
August 1981

1
Starting Out Right

1. Encounter with Destiny

For new employees, entering a company is like an encounter with destiny. On one level, it is the convergence of choice and chance, a fortuitous meeting of their aspirations and the firm's selection process. For his or her part, the freshman employee made a deliberate choice among options, doubtless with the guidance and counsel of parents, teachers, and older friends. The company, for its part, concluded that "this is the kind of person we need," and offered a position to that applicant instead of some other. Because conscious decisions made by the employer and prospective employee happened to overlap, the job-hunter is now positioned to launch a career.

Not every young person is accepted by their employer of first choice, however, and not every company can hire exactly the kind of person it wants for each position. Clearly, therefore, when the two are brought together to realize their compatibility, there is some much greater, subtler force at work than the coincidence of decisions made by employer and recruit. I call that force destiny.

Destiny is an unseen agent that, in part, determines our lives, independent of individual will or desire. To be born in Japan, the United States, or wherever, to be raised as Japanese or Americans, and to carry on with one's life and career in whatever country, is destiny. We had no choice in the matter. Whether we are born Japanese, Australian, or Filipino is the work of destiny, an unknown over which we have no influence at all. We have to accept it. It seems to me that a new employee also should regard his or her employment in a certain company as only partly the outcome of personal volition and consider it in a larger frame as part of the fulfillment of individual destiny.

Notions like destiny might seem quaint, but I believe that the idea can become a source of great strength to people in routine work and in their careers. As a new employee, you face tough decisions and painful dilemmas in the years ahead, especially if you are promoted to a position of responsibility with others under your supervision. These difficulties are a part of any corporate endeavor. The important issue is how you deal with problems, whether you let them defeat you, or whether you find a way to overcome them and continue to grow.

When problems begin to weigh on your mind, it helps to be aware of the role of destiny. It is easier to tackle your difficulties with courage and conviction if you accept their inevitability. What looked like insurmountable problems can turn into challenges to be overcome in the process of your growth and self-improvement.

Employees who are able to confront and surmount these challenges are a valuable asset to their companies. Whether or not they develop the capacity to work creatively despite adversity depends heavily on the individual's original attitude toward his or her job. Those who recognize the hand of destiny in their employment respond much more effectively to the day-to-day difficulties encountered in the workplace.

2. Growth Begins with Trust

For new employees, trust in the company is essential. No amount of prior knowledge can fully prepare you for dealing with the new tasks, situations, and personalities that one finds in any new context. In this totally unfamiliar environment, fundamental trust in one's employer makes it far easier to relax and get down to work.

It helps to remember that neither a company nor its employees are likely to take a malevolent attitude toward a brand new worker. On the contrary, they should welcome him or her with high expectations and willingly give instruction and advice. Indeed, an employer is eager to have a new employee grow accustomed to working in the company as quickly as possible, and makes serious efforts to help the newcomer develop the necessary skills. An employee's potential would be wasted if he or she were simply left to drift from one payday to the next. The employee would be bored and the company disappointed. It is in the company's best interests that new recruits continue to learn and grow, and the staff will offer as much encouragement and support as possible. For a company to neglect the training and education of new employees is to abdicate its responsibilities. Such a firm is unlikely to grow and be successful.

The responsibility of a company to train its members ultimately derives from the expectations of society. A corporation is called upon to fulfill demands from a number of sources, including the consumers, the nation, and in the broadest sense, the world. Unless it trains all of its employees properly and helps them to grow as people, it cannot hope to meet those demands adequately.

In a normal, healthy enterprise, new employees can be assured that their superiors and co-workers fully support their efforts to improve and advance. The surest path to success in business is to maintain from the start the determination to "grow as a dedicated employee of the company and contribute to society through work."

3. One Simple Key to Success

Over the years I have learned something that may seem trivial but could actually affect your promotions and entire career in a company. Very simply, it revolves around the attitude you go home with after your first day at the office.

Day number one is normally spent carrying out formalities: introductions to the president and other executives; a guided tour of the premises; learning about the general rules and procedures of the office. When you get home, invariably someone will ask you about your impressions. I argue that your response may be crucial to your future in the firm.

Success or failure in a career depends to a large extent on attitude. Positive enthusiasm suggests that you will give your best effort to the job. A negative or condescending attitude often means that you give up before you have really started, certainly a prescription for failure. Be enthusiastic, and be sure to communicate that enthusiasm to your family and friends. This will reassure them that you have made a good choice, and they will find it easier to support you in your career. If you are negative or noncommittal, your family will only worry. Their anxiety itself will affect your attitude toward the job and impede your chances for success.

Perhaps it seems unimportant and unnecessary to verbalize your initial reactions, but I truly believe that if you cannot express enthusiasm from the outset, you will find your path very rough indeed. It is not enough to assume that family or friends can guess how you are feeling. You need to articulate it. If you are firmly convinced that you have definitely picked the wrong employer, that is another matter. But if your expectations have not been wholly betrayed, you should be able to say, "Everything's okay; all I have to do is work hard." To be able to reply in that spirit to your family's questions, and indeed to yourself, after the first day is the first step to a successful career.

Your enthusiasm will also have a ripple effect on your company's success. Friends and relatives will be interested when they ask how you like your new job. If you reply, "I'm really pleased to be with such a good company" and list the many ways it suits you, they will perk up their ears. To hear you declare that you are happy to be committing your career to the company that hired you will leave an impression. They may be more inclined to try its products. With such encounters as a catalyst, the name and reputation of the company will spread, sales will rise, and more business will be generated. The firm's growth will promote your own career, and it all starts with your reaction on the day you started work.

Even though it is a simple exercise, surprisingly the majority of employees seldom praise or express loyalty to their company. During my many years in business, I met countless people in other firms who were always able to complain about their work in one way or another. I have encountered only a few individuals willing to declare that they believed in their company and would continue to work wholeheartedly for its growth.

Nothing constructive ever comes from grumbling. On the contrary, those people who speak positively and confidently about their place of employment are the ones whom management notices. They are in great demand and are considered to be valuable assets. These are the people who are singled out for promotion. Honest praise for your company is a key to success. I can say this categorically, but the most convincing proof is to try it yourself.

4. Getting the Most Out of a Teacher

Those in charge of instructing new employees are management and staff personnel who have been with the company for some time. They include people of all types. Some are admirable not only for their character and performance, but also for skill in passing on their wisdom and knowledge to newcomers. Others may be difficult to work with and inept at guiding and encouraging others.

Most people would argue that the first type become better teachers. In any endeavor, it seems common logic that the best way to advance is to find a teacher whose character is exemplary and who is a skilled instructor. People go to great pains searching for a teacher with these qualities when they need help learning something. That is natural; certainly it is desirable to be taught by someone known to be skilled in instructing others and who is considerate and understanding. Yet even the most sympathetic and experienced teachers do not necessarily produce the best results. Students need to be challenged to transcend their limits. With a sensitive and competent teacher the student will often be content to learn what is taught rather than push on to break new ground.

We often hear stories of brilliant artists or other outstanding achievers in a given field who were trained by difficult or impossible taskmasters. Typically, they rarely heard a word of praise during their training, no matter how commendable their performance. Receiving nothing but harsh words and criticism, time after time they hovered on the brink of giving up. People who can endure this treatment and persevere often acquire a highly tempered skill that eventually leads them beyond their teachers to earn great renown. It is fascinating to me how human beings, facing the obstacles before them, refine their abilities to transcend their perceived limitations.

There is no denying the advantages of learning under the tutelage of a considerate teacher. For one thing, the learning process is much more pleasant. To have such a teacher is good fortune. It is no cause for despair, however, if your teacher or superior is unsympathetic, cold, or unskilled. It is, rather, a challenge. First, accept the situation, then approach it as a chance to stretch your abilities. In the process of overcoming the difficulties, you may find yourself moving toward your goals.

5. Know Your Company's History

History is an invaluable guide. As citizens of a country, we should know something of our national history and traditions. An understanding of our nation's origins and development can help us form goals for ourselves in our own time and decide what we want for our country in the future.

In the same way, the history of a company is important to its employees. They need to know about its past in order to contribute effectively in the present. Even the biggest corporations of today were not that way from the beginning. A firm now in its 30th year started out three decades ago from nothing but the determination and ambition of one person or one group. The efforts of the founders, their successors, and other employees over the years have made it what it is today.

Every enterprise accumulates a vast store of experience upon which the present generation builds. We tend to be oriented toward the present condition of and future improvements in the company, often forgetting that progress is rooted in the foundations of the past. A newcomer's first task, therefore, should be to learn about his or her firm's history—how it started and what previous generations accomplished. Without understanding that background, a new employee cannot contribute much.

Furthermore, today's new employees will in two, five, or ten years, be instructing tomorrow's new recruits. They will find that familiarity with the company history provides the basis to speak with authority and conviction about what the organization is and where it is headed. Only if they learn the lessons drawn from their organization's history will they be able to pass them on to younger workers just coming in.

6. Good Manners Help Relationships

"Young people just don't seem to know their manners anymore." This is a complaint that one hears with some frequency at the office and in general conversation.

As a blanket generalization, of course, it is simply false, for there are many young people who are well-mannered and carefully observe the rules of proper decorum. Nonetheless, it is also true that over the past four decades or so there has been, in Japan and other advanced industrial nations as well, a gradual relaxation of the rather strict codes of discipline that prevailed heretofore in the home and in the schools. The image of parents and teachers as friends has partially displaced their function as authority figures. It is quite natural, therefore, that an increasing number of young adults have a more casual attitude toward social etiquette than earlier generations.

Entering the corporate environment can be a bit of a shock for such free spirits; for despite the many changes in society, good manners are still a fundamental social requirement, especially in business. They may find the etiquette demanded of them in formal situations, in this highly structured setting stiff and unnatural. But it is hard to deny that good manners are important in society. Even young people who have never given much thought to manners feel uncomfortable when they encounter insolence or discourtesy directed at them or someone close to them.

Yet "good manners" need be neither uncomfortably stiff nor overly formal. I prefer to think of etiquette as a lubricant that helps the wheels of social interaction turn smoothly. Trying to live and work with each other without common courtesy is like trying to operate machinery without sufficient lubrication; friction builds, sparks fly, and the machine itself begins to break down. We have to keep our human interactions as well oiled as our machines.

When people who differ in age, gender, and basic outlook on life work together in a common endeavor, conflicts can arise. A shared code of good manners provides the rules and structures that allow disparate individuals to resolve potential conflicts and deal with obstacles in a unified way. True courtesy is sincere and explicit; otherwise its effect is lost. Thus, for the company to function smoothly, the new employee needs to acquire as quickly as possible conventional workplace manners that combine both sincerity and correct form.

7. Staying Healthy Is Part of the Job

Mental and physical health are a working person's most valuable assets. No matter how much talent you have, it is of little use to you or your company if you fall ill and cannot perform adequately. During my many years in business, I watched many young employees leave their jobs because of poor health. Such developments were unfortunate for the company, but even more for the individuals concerned. They had to abandon their hopes and expectations for a career in business, all because of poor health.

Most firms make efforts to see that their employees stay healthy. Some provide company health care and fitness programs, or other recreation facilities, but it is we ourselves who must learn how to maintain and improve our state of health. We need to watch the way we eat, get adequate rest, and exercise moderately, but experience has taught me that a healthy state of mind is equally important. The Japanese saying, "Illness begins in the mind," is often correct.

When a person feels well and happy, he or she doesn't tire easily and tends not to get sick. Consider sports or hobby enthusiasts. Absorbed in those activities, they don't seem even weary long after someone else would be exhausted. What is tiring to one person is exhilarating to another. Enjoyment seems to suspend fatigue.

The same is true when you approach work with positive enthusiasm. Totally involved, you hardly notice if your schedule is packed, or if you have to work through the night now and then. Those who enjoy their jobs can work long and hard without getting run down or sick. If you are unenthusiastic or half-hearted about your work, on the other hand, you are more likely to tire easily or be frequently ill.

The crux of staying fit is to know your limits and strike an optimum balance. The human body cannot be used and abused indefinitely. Be careful not to let the pressure of work get out of control, and don't immerse yourself so deeply in your job that you become a victim of overwork, mentally or physically. Strive to maintain a positive frame of mind and keep fit in ways that suit you. Remember that maintaining good health is part of your job.

8. Be Tactful, but Speak Up

New employees learn the ropes with the help and guidance of their superiors and more experienced colleagues. It is important that they listen carefully to what they are told, always asking questions to clarify any given point. This is part of the ongoing process of becoming full-fledged, competent members of the company.

Being a novice, however, should not mean always being passive. There is nothing wrong with bringing up questions or mentioning problems that bother you from the very beginning. Freshman employees, low in status and still feeling unsure of themselves, often hesitate to offer any proposals or ideas of their own. Not wanting to appear presumptuous, they tend only to do what they are told. From the point of view of the company, however, such reticence wastes time and talent. Since the goal of the company is to grow and improve, everyone's ideas are valuable, even those of the greenest recruit.

Senior employees may possess more experience and know-how, but they are also more likely to cling to the old ways rather than try new directions that deserve to be explored. In contrast, newcomers have a fresh perspective, and may be able to see how improvements could be made. I always urge new employees to trust their judgment and speak up if they have ideas they wish to share.

Of course, a new idea must be put forward with tact and consideration for the feelings of your colleagues, especially your seniors. But if, after thinking about it, you believe it will be useful, you should not hesitate to take the initiative and present it with confidence.

For their part, the more experienced members of a company should try to create an environment in which new employees will feel comfortable offering their ideas and opinions. Everyone should be encouraged to consider proposals that are sound, regardless of who put them forward. In such an environment, the company and all its members, new and old, will thrive.

9. Give the Job a Chance

A cold, hard rock is not usually a place one chooses to sit for very long. But an old Japanese maxim advises us that even a rock will begin to feel warm and comfortable if you "sit on it for three years" (*ishi no ue ni mo sannen*). The message is clear: patience and perseverance are all-important, something a new employee should remember as he or she takes up the challenges of a new job.

Younger people tend to be impatient. Some decide they don't like the work and quit after only a month or two. As long as jobs are plentiful and varied, and they are serious in finding the vocation that suits their abilities, they may find another, more satisfying position. In reality, however, it takes more than a few months to know whether a job is right for you or not, no matter what kind of work it is.

Often a job that didn't interest you at all at first begins to grow more congenial after a few years and you begin to show an increasing aptitude for the work. The longer you persevere at it, the more your job intrigues you. In many cases, as the proverb suggests, it takes about three years before you really appreciate the work you are engaged in.

When I was a young man, patience and perseverance were valued more highly than they are today. People rarely quit a job within only a few years of being hired. Granted, the job-hunter had fewer options than today, and the variety of available jobs was narrower. But people were also more inclined to persist in situations that initially might have seemed intolerable, supported by the belief that time would bring its own rewards. Many of us did learn, in fact, to appreciate our jobs more than we did when we started out.

No matter how much the content and methods of work may have changed, I believe that patience and perseverance are still important. Whatever career or occupation you have chosen, you should stick with it for at least three years. Unwillingness to commit enough time to give your decision a chance indicates lack of confidence in your own ability to choose. If, even after three years, you are convinced the job is not right for you, the experience it provided will still be valuable.

New employees often wonder whether the job they have chosen is really right for them. It is a perfectly natural question to which I would respond that Japan's age-old wisdom supplies the best answer. Sit tight and see if the rock grows more comfortable.

10. Shouldering Your Share of the Load

Speaking to a group of young employees, I once discussed the relationship between work and salary. I admitted that I received the largest paycheck in the company, but I added,

"I always strive to produce at least ten times that much in my work." Just starting out, a young employee might assume that he or she only has to produce an amount equivalent to their own salary, but that's not how a company works. A business as a whole must produce much more than the equivalent of all salaries, just to survive. As a rule of thumb, each employee needs to earn at least three times his or her salary in order to keep the enterprise viable, and if possible ten times.

A company needs funds above and beyond salary requirements to invest in plant and equipment, give dividends to shareholders, and pay the taxes that keep our government solvent, among others. If all employees understand the value of their work in this way, it will enhance their performance and stimulate their best efforts. Their combined endeavors will open new frontiers and fill a company with tremendous dynamism.

I cannot overemphasize this point. We all work hard at our jobs, but it is not enough just to have a vague sense that one is working hard. Even though it is not always easy to calculate the worth of work in terms of money, we must realize that the value of our work is measured not by the size of our paychecks. It is measured by the concrete results we achieve for the company, and ultimately by the benefits they generate for society as a whole.

11.　The Company as "Public Institution"

Everyone has personal motives and goals when he or she begins a career in business. For some, employment offers a chance to advance knowledge or skills, to use their talents in a particular field, or to travel and work abroad. Some set their sights on the top of the executive ladder; others are content just to make a decent living. Whatever your motives and expectations, one thing all employees should understand about the purpose of work is that the corporation as well as the jobs in it are, in the final analysis, part of the public domain.

A company cannot conduct its operations in isolation, for it is an integral part of the social and economic fabric. Depending on the nature of its activities and its performance, it will have either a positive or a negative impact on the community as a whole. A company that inhibits rather than enhances the well-being of society has lost its primary reason for existence. Making a positive contribution to the society in which it operates should be the ultimate goal for every company.

The same is true of the work of each employee. No job is really "yours" in the sense that you are free to go about it as you alone see fit. The social obligations of the company as a whole are borne, in turn, by every employee in every daily task they perform, particularly senior employees. It is important that everyone in the organization, brand new recruits included, realize that their responsibilities extend much farther than the company itself.

2
Compass for Experience

1. Boss as Client

One of my favorite pieces of advice for white collar corporate employees is that they approach their job the same way they would if they were independent entrepreneurs. I think that, in some ways, every employee must operate as though she or he were the manager of a business. Someone who belongs to the accounting department of a company, for example, should handle their duties like the director of an accounting firm.

How you regard your role has an impact on business because it affects your attitude and behavior. By visualizing yourself as an executive in charge of an enterprise, you are more likely to find ways to streamline operations and enhance your performance. You see yourself as important rather than as just one cog in the wheels of an immense corporation. You savor the challenges of each day's labors and gain fulfillment from your accomplishments. Naturally you cannot expect your initiatives to produce immediate returns in terms of higher pay or other privileges. Instead you treat your salary as the stipend you receive from the running of your "business."

If in your own mind you are the head of your own business, your co-workers and superiors are your company's "clientele." Businesses provide a variety of services to their regular patrons; the sales force in a shop, for instance, will warmly welcome a customer and bring out appropriate items to show. They may invite the visitor to sit down and have a cup of tea while they lay out the latest wares and talk about the business. You should treat your boss and colleagues in a similar fashion.

When you think of new ideas or innovations, share them with your associates, section or department chief, or even your company president. It may take some salesmanship on your part to persuade them that the "goods" you offer will make a contribution, but if you are successful and they try your suggestion, you will have the pleasure of seeing it put into practice. Your "enterprise" will thrive and you will derive greater satisfaction from your work. If all the employees in a corporation show the same spirit, moreover, the energy it generates will give the organization as a whole a unique dynamism.

2. Love Your Work

Upon taking a job, some people aggressively pursue the assignments they want. When they are hired, they make a point of stating the kind of work they really like and feel best suited for and they request being used in that capacity. Some employers try to place them according to their preferences, but I do not think this happens very often. Ordinarily management simply dictates their jobs. Aptitude may be taken into account, but more often other factors have greater priority.

Whether you get your preferred assignment or not, most important is the attitude with which you accept and perform the task you are given. There are options. You can resign yourself in stony silence to a job you dislike, develop no particular interest in it, and derive no fulfillment from it. You simply go through the motions. Speaking out, you might declare yourself unsuited to the job and ask to have your assignment changed. Neither of these is a good solution, for you gain nothing from your work if you are simply resigned to it, and your potential will never be tested if you avoid the unfamiliar at every turn. Lacking interest in your work drains your incentive and the job quickly tires you out, mentally and physically. This is not the image of a satisfied, productive worker.

Ideally, one wants to be working at a job he or she enjoys. Some people claim to compensate for distasteful or boring jobs by active outside interests, and certainly everyone needs some kind of activity that provides a change of pace. I am convinced, however, that you cannot find genuine pleasure in recreational pursuits unless your daily labors on the job are truly satisfying.

You need to get the most out of your work, therefore, both for its own sake and to enjoy the other areas of your life. That requires a deliberate effort to discover what intrinsic interest the job may hold. For example, perhaps you are unhappy with the task assigned to you; you have asked to be shifted else-where, only to be told, "This experience will be valuable to you in the future, so stick with it for at least a year." In a case like this, it is worth analyzing why your employer picked you instead of somebody else for that particular task. If you can set aside your resistance long enough to understand the reason, it may be easier, even challenging, to accept the assignment and carry it through.

Some jobs turn out to be intolerable, no matter what you do. But most of the time, work is a creative process. Imagination and ingenuity will help you find ways to cope with tasks that are hard for you or unpleasant. As your efforts begin to be appreciated, you'll find yourself growing interested in the work after all. You should always hope your work is so absorbing that it even appears in your dreams.

3. Know-How Is Not Everything

Many years ago Henry Ford complained that even his best technicians always seemed to be bristling with theories about what could *not* be done. Ford was an inventor. He needed engineers and technicians to put his inventions, like the conveyor belt assembly-line system, to work in his factories. Later, however, he recalled that most of the time they would declare flat out, "It can't be done. It's impossible. Theoretically, it's not workable." He found that the more technologically sophisticated the consultant, the more often this was the response. In the end, Ford's innovative genius won out over their theoretical conservatism.

Ford's experience reminds me of the Japanese penchant to mistrust theories, to derogate the "weakness of the intellectual." Why do we associate the intellectual with weakness? Should not a person who has acquired considerable knowledge and information be expected to be that much stronger? Most endeavors cannot even be attempted without a certain level of factual knowledge, techniques, or procedures.

Perhaps Ford's dilemma and the Japanese adage reflect what happens when people let their knowledge—especially theoretical—and information get in the way of creativity. Given a task, people generally plunge right in without worrying too much about the whys and wherefores. With energy and ingenuity, even difficult projects can be completed quite successfully.

Too much prior information, on the other hand, can be inhibiting. We become convinced that "I can't do this; it's too difficult." Before we even try, we are defeated—hamstrung by our own knowledge. That is the handicap encapsulated in the phrase "weakness of the intellectual."

As more young people seek higher levels of education, new employees tend increasingly to be high school and university graduates. A better educated work force means a stronger work force in an age when the increasing complexity of society, work, and technology demands competent, well-informed people. But we must not be *confined* by the knowledge we have acquired. When a job lies before you, it is best simply to start in and get to work, without thinking too hard about it. Once you understand what is practically required, you can draw on your fund of knowledge to revise and complete the task thoroughly and efficiently. At that stage your book-learning and theoretical know-how will be assets, instead of liabilities.

Fresh out of college, perhaps you may be steeped in the academic approach, in the use of knowledge for its own sake; you think theory holds unlimited promise, while practice is only derivative, mundane. Sometimes, however, a more practical, intuitive perspective is not only more successful, but necessary. As long as you keep that in mind, knowledge will be a source of strength, not weakness.

4. Learn to Follow Through

Trust is created by demonstrating dependability, responsibility, and by maintaining maximum communication. Suppose I ask a subordinate to contact someone and cancel an appointment. I add, "Please ask him if he wouldn't mind postponing our meeting until tomorrow." The employee almost automatically answers, "Yes, sir, I'll attend to it right away," and will put the call through. So far, so good, but what next? Some people will leave it at that, but others will follow through on the matter, and come back to report, "I made the call, and Mr. X says that tomorrow will be fine." That last step may not seem worth the bother, but it can make a reputation or break it.

Once you have requested that something be done, you have to assume it will be, but you can't be sure nor can you know what the outcome was unless you receive a proper report. Without confirmation, the matter might still be hanging, but engulfed by a busy schedule, you don't have time to check. If the person you asked will just stop by your office and say, "About that call—tomorrow's fine," you don't have to worry about it and can go on with your business. Cumulatively, such simple, final reports can take a lot of pressure off a boss's day.

The same is true if a client asks you to give a message to the person in your company in charge of their account. You pass on the message, but if you then call the client back and confirm that it was received, he or she will know the communication has been completed. This service is generally not expected, but it is tremendously appreciated.

It is the small considerate acts, I believe, that reassure people. They develop confidence in you, and help build your reputation as someone who is competent and can be trusted. Intelligence and capability are important, but close attention to details can determine the way you are regarded.

A person who will take on difficult, complex tasks but won't bother with the more mundane details can be more trouble than help. Actually the ordinary, inglorious tasks are the essential ones, and so the best route to a solid career is to start by becoming familiar with the simpler aspects of the job. From there, you can go on to gain more experience and apply your skills and know-how to work more and more extensively.

This advice applies not just to younger employees, but to everyone, from department chief to the temporary staff who run errands. Those who can be trusted the most are always the ones who follow up every request with a report, whether the task was performed successfully or not. If a department chief knows that everything in his domain is going well, for example, there might be nothing in particular to tell his superior. The greater the understanding between management staff and their head, the easier it is to decide when an update or casual report will set the boss's mind at rest and keep the channels of communication open, for good news or bad. A person skilled in handling the small matters of a business has taken the first step to earning the solid trust of clients and to becoming indispensable to the company.

5. Cultivating Good Instincts

People in business soon learn how important it is to be alert to problems and opportunities that come up, not only in their own sphere of responsibility, but in other areas as well. It takes time and practice to develop the ability to react smoothly and instinctively in any situation. Let me share a story from my own experience to illustrate what I mean.

I wanted to talk with the president of a certain company, but when I called, I was told he was away on business and wouldn't be back for several days. There was nothing I could do but wait until his return, I thought. I was about to hang up when the person on the other end said, "Just a moment. If it's something urgent, I can get in touch with him for you." Learning that the president could be contacted without great difficulty, I requested that he call me back that evening. When he phoned me long distance a few hours later I was able to settle the matter and get it out of the way, thanks to the quick thinking of his subordinate.

This was not an earth-shaking event, but such a response even in minor matters can make all the difference in running a business. The ability to deal with people and events on the spur of the moment with consideration and good judgment is very important. I could tell that the person I was speaking to had that ability, learned under a boss who was strict about the way his employees treated people and used the telephone. Clearly his assistant knew what to do in the kind of situation my call presented. In times like ours, hours or even minutes can be crucial in cinching a transaction or making a key decision. Employees must be able to exercise this kind of discretion and respond smoothly to people's needs with sensitivity and thoughtfulness.

It is one thing to know what you ought to do and another to put that knowledge into practice. Since you never know what you might be called upon to do, you need to hone your instincts regarding the proper manners and procedures in the day-to-day course of events. Ultimately, that is the only way to be certain that you are well equipped to deal with the unexpected.

6. Self-Improvement

In 1965, about six months after we shifted to the five-day workweek at Matsushita Electric Industrial, I spoke to employees about our shared responsibility to the company and society to improve ourselves. Now that we only work five days a week, I said, "What guides you in allocating your time during the two days off? Are you using the time effectively, one day for rest and the other for self-improvement?" I expressed my hope that, rather than simply idling away their weekends, they were making efforts to better themselves, physically or mentally, or both.

I knew that many of my employees were using the time to study or learn new hobbies or skills, acquire training to enhance their performance at work, and/or undertake health and fitness programs. I then asked, "Whatever you are doing during your weekends, have you considered that self-improvement benefits more than just yourself? Are you aware that it is your responsibility as a member of society?"

I believe very strongly that a company employee must be bound by a sense of responsibility to society. It goes without saying that we will benefit from any efforts we make to increase our ability or knowledge, or to upgrade our work performance. But the pursuit of such benefits is itself an obligation to society. After all, every step forward that each of us takes carries our society that much further ahead. But if you take only one step while everyone else has taken three, in effect you are holding back the entire society. Enriching your mind, enhancing your skills, and building a healthy body should not be undertaken simply to gain personal happiness or higher status. These individual endeavors are the common responsibility of all of us as members of our society. In the final analysis, to study or not to study is more than a purely personal choice; we have to think beyond ourselves. Living up to these responsibilities, I reminded the group, is an affirmation of solidarity with other members of society.

7. Vocation and Avocation

A hobby can be a distraction from your work, or it can be an advantage. Some people describe their work as simply what they do for a living and say their real sense of fulfillment comes from their hobby. They will probably have trouble making a success of their careers. Unless your work deeply interests you and provides some measure of enjoyment, you will not get the most out of it.

Suppose you are an office worker but find yourself so wrapped up in writing poetry, playing the guitar, or some other hobby, that you cannot get it out of your mind. Every time you sit down to tally up figures or prepare reports, you begin composing verses or strumming songs in your head instead. For you, such preoccupations are far more interesting and satisfying than any job you are assigned at the office. If that is your situation, you should think seriously about quitting your company and taking up poetry writing or guitar as a full-time occupation.

In the past anyone who made such a decision would have had to be willing to put up with near starvation in order to devote themselves full time to poetry, music, or whatever. Nonetheless some accepted the challenge. Today, fortunately, one needn't court starvation to follow one's dreams. So if you happen to find more fulfillment in such an occupation than in being office worker, then by all means, give it a try. You ought to be willing to trade some of the comforts of a company environment for the freedom to pursue a vocation that will give your life a real sense of purpose, even if it means being somewhat poorer.

For other people, however, work is their main calling, the vocation to which they have devoted their lives. For these people, poetry or guitar are hobbies for their spare time, diversions that provide personal enrichment and cultivate sensibility and creativity. I believe most people view their hobbies this way, as supporting, complementary activities to work, rather than potential vocations. Whatever you decide, it is important that the work you do be the occupation that gives you the most personal satisfaction and fulfillment.

8. How to Sell Ability

Selling a product, whether it is a commodity or some kind of service, can be very difficult. In some rare cases, a product will sell merely on the strength of good advertising, but usually much more persuasion is also required. A person who makes sales a profession is constantly devising new tactics and using them on the job.

Effective sales technique is a vital skill, not only for the salesperson, but for any employee. Convincing your supervisors or your close colleagues to adopt a proposal you have designed for a project depends in part on the suitability of the proposal itself, but also on how persuasively you can "sell" it to them. In other words, among a businessman's most valuable skills is knowing how to present an idea in such a way that the boss will say, "This is a splendid proposal. We'll put it to work right away."

Furthermore, inadequate sales technique on your part can undermine your relationships on the job. If you take no interest in how to sell things or ideas and exercise no imagination when you present some project, chances are it will not be adopted. In turn, you will perceive your superiors as unsympathetic and close-minded, unable to see the merits of your idea. That kind of attitude does nothing to help you or your company grow.

In commercial sales, the quality of the merchandise is naturally the most important factor, but even the finest products will not sell well if they are presented clumsily or in poor taste. By the same token, employees need to "sell" themselves, to convince others of their worth in order to advance. Experience and ability are the most important factor in employee performance, and workers have to make continual efforts to improve their qualifications. At the same time, developing the skills to "sell" your ability in a way that helps others understand what you can do is basic to a successful career in business.

9. The Function of Reprimands

No one likes to be taken to task for making mistakes or misjudgments. It can ruin your whole day to be called in and reprimanded by the boss. People generally prefer not to be told off, even when they have obviously made an error or bungled an assignment. Having to deliver severe words leaves a bad aftertaste for supervisors, too. Any manager knows how unpleasant it is to rebuke employees.

But what would happen if both sides avoided the disagreeable confrontation with the matter and left it unmentioned? The boss's irritation at mistakes that cost the company money or damaged its reputation would fester and the employee's contrition would remain unexpressed. Even one problem left unsettled and undiscussed can snowball, leading to more difficulties. In such cases, both employee and manager can risk letting the tension and toughness required for successful business go slack and their thinking can become soft and undisciplined. When people start to take the easy way out, they stop trying hard. If they are members of an organization, and they relax the demands on themselves, their performance suffers. In the worst scenario, they sooner or later face corporate bankruptcy.

Individual autonomy is valued much more today than it used to be. Employees are given wider latitude to adopt their own pace and patterns of working, but this does not mean that rebukes and reprimands are no longer needed. In fact, the more we accept autonomy and individuality on the job, the clearer it should be that what molds strength and competence is firm discipline. When I was young and was head of our factory, I often scolded my employees. In those days, the company was growing at full steam, and I was never so gentle as to call someone into my office for a quiet talk. I let them have it right there in front of the whole workshop, raising my voice and pounding the table.

My explosions may have been blistering, but they left no one in a state of depression. On the contrary, my employees actually took pride in this treatment. It indicated that I cared about their work, and that I knew they were tough. We were relatively small at the very beginning, but as the company grew and the number of employees increased, I couldn't stop and critique the work or remonstrate with each and every one who made a mistake. So when I found something wrong, I ended up directing my observations at a supervisor. Workers were so seldom scolded directly by me that they began saying around the workshop, "If the Captain (that was what they called me in those days) lights into you, you've made it." In other words, the boss trusted you.

51

After I'd given somebody a dressing down, he'd glow with the somewhat embarrassing recognition of what it meant. His co-workers would pat him on the back, the lucky one the Captain took the trouble to "call on the carpet." Being scolded is usually a painful experience, but they had a positive attitude about it that, I believe, provided much impetus to the growth of each employee and the company as a whole.

If a person does a sloppy job and no one appears to care, he or she can assume that a mediocre performance is good enough and stop trying to improve. When that happens workers cease to grow or progress, depriving the individual employee, the company, and the society of the benefits of their best efforts. When the situation demands a severe reprimand, it should be delivered right away, with energy and conviction. To be able to accept the rebuke with humility and an open mind can become a springboard to further growth and better performance. I think this applies equally to both younger employees and persons in positions of responsibility. Young people in particular should try to regard the occasion of a reprimand as a milestone marking their progress in the world of business.

10. Worth Your Very Life

How many people could you find in business these days willing to say they would stake their lives on their career? The vast majority would probably be shocked at the thought. As I see it, however, nothing could be more splendid than to be engaged in work that means so much to you that you would risk your life for it. I think, in fact, that one shouldn't expect true success in anything without that degree of commitment.

The Soviet cosmonaut Yuri Gagarin, the first man to travel in outer space, made his voyage in 1961, a time when an astronaut's life was definitely on the line. Every possible precaution was taken to insure his safe return, but there were a great many unknown factors and the dangers were real. Gagarin was willing to try—to stake his life, literally, on his work—and his brave mission placed the Soviet Union in the vanguard of space travel. If he had refused, protesting, "Absolutely not. It's too dangerous; there's no way I'll go up there!" he would have sacrificed a magnificent success. The same is true for the astronauts in the more recent flights of the American Space Shuttle.

The work of an astronaut is an extreme example, but it illustrates the kind of spirit we need in our work day-to-day to achieve success. The employees of a company, especially the younger ones who are full of energy and drive, should throw themselves into their work with the same zeal that Gagarin demonstrated. Their devotion will increase the fulfillment and enjoyment they gain from their work, and just as important, it will draw the attention of their co-workers. Such committed, focused concentration on the part of one is contagious, and helps to build a strong foundation for a prosperous company.

Sometimes dedication backfires. The person in an organization willing to stake his or her life on their work can inspire resentment. Jealous accusations of "impertinence" or egotism may begin to circulate. This tendency is an unfortunate remnant of outdated traditions that dictated strict conformity and uniformity. It goes against all the ideals of democracy we have sought so hard to cultivate. If we truly treasure democratic ideals, we should encourage ambition and talent, not suppress or ridicule them. Democracy functions at its best

53

when each of us recognizes the strengths of others and cooperates in encouraging and developing them. That way capable people can devote themselves to their work with courage and determination, without having to fear the arrows of collegial jealousy.

Finally, even if you gamble your life on a job, I can think of almost no instance where you will actually lose it. The sincerity of your commitment will, on the contrary, fill you with buoyant energy and only add to your joy of living.

11. Celebrate Talent

A company with one hundred employees should have at least one or two people of outstanding ability who gradually prove to be among the finest assets a company has. As they move into key positions, their impact causes the firm's performance to surge forward. People like this should be prized in any organization, and yet there is often a tendency to envy their achievements. Older employees in particular are sometimes threatened by newer talent.

I once knew of a company of medium size that was doing only tolerably well when its management decided to expand, and it took the ambitious step of hiring ten more employees. Among the ten, two turned out to have unusual ability, and the president promoted them without regard to seniority. The company already had a number of very experienced, long-term employees, but few of them were familiar with the latest technology and information. The two newcomers enjoyed the lavish attention of the president because of the fresh knowledge they brought to the establishment.

A case like this can involve very sensitive human relations problems. Workers are generally not amused to see just one or two of their cohorts receive special notice. But in this company, because of the president's skillful handling, no particular jealousy or resentment was generated among the employees. The two newcomers were rapidly promoted to important positions, and within three years the company had completely remodelled itself and had grown immensely. I have seen this transformation take place in many other companies, demonstrating how extremely valuable the talents of one or two people can be, and how their presence can bring benefits to all the other employees.

The importance of valuing and rewarding merit is recognized more widely in industry today than in the past, although I do not think it is practiced as actively and consistently as it should be. The merit system is hindered in part by seniority-conscious Japanese, who have an ingrained aversion to singling out individuals in accordance with their performance and ability. The person set in a traditional mold does not empathize but is jealous and mean-spirited instead. These feelings, if not dealt with, inevitably taint the atmosphere of the workplace. In such an environment, promotion outside the seniority system can actually obstruct corporate growth and prevent employees from developing their potential.

Recognizing and encouraging outstanding ability is important not just within the corporate context, but throughout our society. We should all strive for greater achievement in our own work, but at the same time we need to support those around us, helping them to develop their talent, rather than trying to hold them down or trip them up out of envy. When a person of unusual ability and wisdom achieves higher positions, he or she will then reach down and pull those along who supported them. In this pattern the entire group grows and improves. More of this willing spirit of cooperation can help our private enterprises, our communities, and our citizenry as a whole.

12. Remember the Excitement

When you are in the doldrums or feeling discouraged by setbacks, it often helps to think back to your first days on the job, when everything about the company was new and fresh to you.

In my case, I started out as a shop apprentice in Osaka, and when I was fifteen or sixteen I decided I wanted a career in the electric business. Through a friend of the family, I was introduced to the Osaka Electric Light Company, then an upcoming firm in the city. I applied for a job and waited. Three months passed and still there was no opening. Thinking that perhaps I should give up, but unwilling to abandon the attempt, I took a temporary job with a cement company. Finally, after four months of waiting, I learned there was a position available and that I could take the required examination. I was overjoyed—an opportunity at last—and delighted when I passed the test.

I will never forget the elation I felt upon being hired for the job I had hoped for. That thrill imparted great energy to my work. I remember having tremendous vitality and drive at the time. It seemed that since I finally had the chance I had waited four months for, I had to work really hard and learn as much as I could. My positive enthusiasm probably helped, but everyone in the company was kind and encouraging, and I rose from assistant wiring technician to installation technician in a matter of four months, a promotion that usually took two to three years.

I'm sure everyone experiences the same kind of excitement as I did when they begin employment with a company or other organization. I believe they will also find that recalling that initial thrill can be a source of great strength as one's career goes on, especially when they fall into a slump.

Two or three years after joining a company, employees often begin to experience doubts about themselves and their work and reach a plateau in their careers. Their confidence and interest flag, and they begin to wonder whether they should stay with the company or go elsewhere. An effective means of getting over this hump, I have found, is to think back to the days when you were starting out and remind yourself of the thrill, the excitement, and the determination you felt then. That recollection alone can be a remarkable antidote to mid-career blues.

13. Tempering the Self

In the United States, when a large company establishes an affiliate or builds an additional factory, the person appointed as its top executive can often, apparently, still be in his thirties. In Japan employees under forty traditionally could not expect to be promoted to anything higher than section chief or manager. But in seminars at Matsushita Electric I used to ask middle-echelon employees if they were prepared for such an opportunity: "Suppose you are in your mid-thirties and your company appoints you as head of the engineering department, foreman of a factory, or even president of a small subsidiary. How would you respond? 'Yes sir, I will prove myself worthy of your trust, and show that I can run a factory that has well-trained workers and makes good products' or 'You can be confident that I will do a good job as president.' If there is anyone who could answer like that, raise your hand."

In a Japanese company, employees in their thirties generally have more than ten years experience. What I wanted to find out was whether they were striving to cultivate within themselves the professional skills and confidence to assume responsibilities and perform as well as their peers in Japan or anywhere else in the world. Japanese are trained to be self-deprecating and unassuming to a fault, so no one raised a hand. I would then say, "You are all models of modesty, but what I really hope is that you each become the kind of person whose hand would go up immediately, even if only in your own mind."

If every day you work with the conscious intention of rising to the top, you probably will. All companies are built by people whose ability, acumen, and hard work win them recognition both within their own organization and in their industry. They are the prime movers in the success of their firms. One reason they can accomplish so much is that they make their job the focus of daily, assiduous efforts to train themselves, polish their skills, and master their work. The workplace is the ultimate training ground, whatever your age or occupation. The great names in the performing arts are people who have outstanding talent, but perhaps more important, are so absorbed in the pursuit of their art that they begrudge the slightest distraction. They seek perfection, the sort of person who spends sleepless nights over a single bad review. They are great performers because they are so deeply committed to their art.

Can all of us say that we give the same dedication to refining our skills and improving our performance in our work? If not, we will never achieve the ability and self-confidence we need to assume positions of responsibility. The forging and tempering of ourselves, both personally and professionally, is a cumulative process that must be sustained day-to-day. In this process we can strengthen our resolve by encouraging and advising each other.

14. Consideration for Your Superiors

"Young man, can you do a shoulder massage?"

"No sir, I can't."

"What, you never massaged your mother or father's shoulders?" said I, surprised.

"No," the young man answered in embarrassment, "At least, not very often."

"Well," I warned him, "that means you won't get very far in business."

This was a dialogue between a young employee and myself many years ago. He was obviously puzzled: what possible connection could there be between getting ahead in business and massage? I tried to explain what I meant.

"Suppose you and your chief are working late at night on a rush project. You are young and able to keep going, but your boss is considerably older and quicker to feel the fatigue. You notice that he seems stiff, uncomfortable. Could you—or would you—offer to massage his shoulders?

"You're in the office and work is work, so you don't have to make such an offer, but it's a gesture the section chief would greatly appreciate. Chances are that he will decline your offer, but he will be grateful for the thoughtfulness. In fact, your gesture may please him more than actually getting a massage.

59

The exchange mellows the atmosphere and he may respond in kind: 'Sorry to keep you so late. You probably had a date tonight.'"

I emphasized, "Thoughtfulness among co-workers is a key ingredient for efficient and fruitful labor. I hope you will try to be considerate of your boss and your colleagues as well, because that effort can only add to the success of your endeavors."

I was not talking about apple-polishing or seeking brownie-points, but the kind of genuine concern that endears people to each other. Now since social mores vary, offering to give a massage may not always be the most appropriate way to express this concern. Nonetheless the point remains clear. Showing the respect you feel for seniors and wanting to bolster someone who is tired are natural sentiments and their interplay is what makes human society run smoothly.

Ulterior motives behind kind words and considerate actions eventually show up. If they are part of a strategy, it will soon be exposed and probably backfire. But if your words and actions are sincere, other people will know and respect you for them. Perhaps I am old-fashioned, but I believe an ability to be considerate in a genuine, natural way can only have positive influence on others, and is in great demand in any workplace.

3
Pointers for Professionals

1. Don't Blame Your Subordinates

When a particular department in a firm chronically fails to perform as expected, top management is likely to call in its head and ask for an explanation. The department chief typically will plead apologetically, "I'm doing my very best. It's the section chiefs. You see, one or two are not really suited to the work and have been making it difficult for the rest of us to do any better. I'm very sorry."

His evaluation of the problem may very well be accurate, but is it right for a manager to evade responsibility this way? Each department has an important function in the company, and the person ultimately responsible for making sure it carries out that function effectively is the chief. If performance lags because some members are not contributing their share to the work, it is the chief's task to find a solution and raise efficiency, even if some members of the staff or crew have to be replaced.

One way of dealing with such problems is to submit a request asking top management to reassign certain staff members to other parts of the company. You can explain that although a particular person might be very capable in another area, he or she seems out of place in your department. In the end, carefully considered changes benefit not just the department, but the employee in question and the company as a whole.

Some department managers would not even contemplate making such a request in fear that it would reflect badly on their management ability. It might be interpreted as evidence that they don't know how to work with subordinates. Actually, an unwillingness to speak out and suggest a necessary change reveals that a chief lacks both a firm sense of his or her role as a manager and a clear vision of the mission that the company—and the department—has to society.

The same principle applies to department chiefs themselves. If you think you are not suited to the post of department chief, you ought to present your case to your president or supervisory officer, speaking for yourself alone. You might say: "I've been chief for a year now but have not been able to improve the department's output. This seems to indicate that I am not the right person to lead it. I'd appreciate it if you would shift me to some other work."

Any judgment about whether you yourself or your subordinates are well placed in a particular job must be as objective as possible, made without prejudice. Once the decision has been made, act on it right away. It may be that both your own career and that of a subordinate will go much more smoothly if given a chance in a different venue.

How well a department is managed depends on the person who heads it; a department chief, in short, cannot pass the buck—either up or down. A company will show steady growth only if all its management staff fully understand the importance of being responsible for their own actions and those of their subordinates, day by day, month by month.

2. Accepting Responsibility

Meetings are often used to get the widest possible input from all concerned parties when a decision has to be made on an important issue. This is a democratic procedure and eminently sensible. But although the decision seems to be made by the group as a whole, it is the manager of the unit that must determine whether to actually implement that decision.

Since the manager makes the final judgment, he or she must accept the ultimate responsibility for the decision. Whoever decides whether a policy or rule is to be implemented is the one who must bear responsibility for it, irrespective of how many people worked on it in the first place. Those in management positions become truly "responsible persons" in their department only if they are ready to accept the accompanying burdens and problems.

Unfortunately, genuinely responsible managers are not very numerous. When something goes wrong, instead of accepting blame as head of the department, they try to place it on their subordinates, saying, "Look, you were all involved in the decision. You are as much at fault as I am."

In a leadership position, you articulate your standpoint on specific issues to your supporting staff. Suppose a decision is made among them on the basis of consensus or majority opinion, and it is not one you could implement in good conscience; you must firmly state your disagreement, giving all reasons why you cannot in good conscience, go along with the decision of the group. If you still can't get them to accept your position, you should consider resigning your post. You could, of course, use your authority as manager to force compliance but this would not be likely to lead to good results. The point is that if you value the responsibility you have as highly as you should, you will have the courage to relinquish it. The kind of manager who would accept a decision he personally finds questionable or dangerous, "since it was made by the whole group," has misconceived what it means to assume managerial responsibility.

Conscientiousness and integrity required of managers who deal with matters relating to the company as a whole as well as in intra-departmental affairs. If an issue involves your sphere of administration, you must express your opinions to the president or directors when necessary. Have the courage of your convictions. Keep firm and follow them through, and you will gain the confidence both of your subordinates and your superiors. You will find, moreover, that such an attitude maximizes your performance at work.

3. Hone Your Prefessional Skills

After you have been with a company for a number of years, you will be given increasingly weighty responsibilities and commensurate status. But the real test of how far you have come is whether you can, with quiet confidence, claim to be a mature professional in the job you do. Although you may have been doing your job for many years, are paid a good salary, and feel generally good about your performance on a day-to-day basis, can you call yourself an expert in your field? If questioned about the level of your professional competence, could you with justification compare yourself to a professional chess player who had attained the rank of grand master? Not many managers could, I fear, but it is crucial to the health of an organization that all employees who reach administrative rank continually strive to acquire the skills and confidence to merit a comparison. Mastery of a field requires both experience and commitment to improving one's skills.

Drawing offers a good example. A beginner finds it difficult to produce a good sketch even though he or she may spend many anguished hours in the attempt, while a highly trained and experienced artist takes pen in hand and without hesitation executes an impressive drawing in a few minutes.

Seasoned skill and experience distinguish the expert from both the neophyte and the hack.

This is true of anything we do in business, whether it is planning, product development, production, or sales. It is the practiced, mature professional who can quickly come up with a workable, intelligent plan or put a product into production speedily. Of course there are times when the ideas are not forthcoming immediately and production takes longer than planned. But you can't allow yourself to rest content with this, thinking that everything is alright as long as the job gets done. A slow response is a sign that you are not yet a master practitioner in your field.

During World War II, many of us were aware of serious flaws in our manufacturing processes. The level of Japan's military technology and expertise was such that when a fault was found in an airplane design, it could take months or even a year before the designs were revised, the problem corrected, and the manufacturing process modified. It was said that in the United States, on the other hand, if a technical problem was discovered in battle, a few technicians would work out a solution, revise the design, and correct the problem within a week, so that week after week, better planes were being sent out against the Japanese forces. This may be apocryphal, but with the proper technology and equipment highly talented designers could well have been able to perform such wonders.

Today, of course, extremely rapid product development and efficient, speedy work are the hallmark of Japanese business. This is only possible because management personnel value and encourage confidence and professional ability. In these times of rapid change, moreover, no one in business can afford to fall behind current trends and developments in their field.

Constant and startling advances in technology threaten to overtake us. Not properly prepared, today's expert can end up being tomorrow's layman. Anyone in a position of responsibility in a company is obligated to continually scrutinize his or her abilities and never stop refining and developing them. With this kind of sustained effort, human ingenuity and the growth of ability have no limits.

4. Keystone of Training

In the long run, the measure of a company's success can be traced to the caliber of its employees. Management's first priority, therefore, is to create a strong workforce. What drives the development of the company as a whole is the performance of each section and department, and better performance comes only with advances in workers' training. That is why employee education should rank very high among the duties of a department chief or section head.

There are many ways to activate the best in a company's human resources. The first step is to establish a set of policies to guide employees in their work. Managers need to set out exactly what the department or section is expected to accomplish and how. They should draw up specific, clearly articulated policies designed to insure that each job can be performed deftly and efficiently. A useful policy reflects a coherent philosophy and should be reiterated often. Employees should be expected to study it carefully and take it seriously. If they have trouble understanding or carrying out any policy, you, the manager, should be willing to provide help and encouragement, and to monitor their responses. This is the most fundamental part of employee training.

Management of the entire corporate entity should be oriented the same way. A president who presents a basic philosophy and articulates the specific policies of the company, asking all members of the firm to work on their skills and train themselves in accordance with stated objectives, is likely to inspire a positive response among employees. They understand what is expected of them and are challenged to live up to it. If a company specifies no policies or it makes no persuasive attempt to rally commitment to such guidelines as it has, the employees will have no clear image of where their work fits into the whole. Not knowing where they are headed, they cannot determine how to proceed. They will work one day at a time, going through the motions, but their abilities and performance may stagnate.

Nations, also, flourish in times when there are clear and attainable goals set before the citizens, and the educational and other institutions are oriented to them. As each citizen works to help achieve the nation's objectives, the country as a whole develops faster. An individual can structure his or her personal life the same way. By setting clear targets and enunciating principles of action, a person can learn to tap great inner resources.

If you are the head of some division in your company, the policies and goals you establish must conform with those of the entire company, and it is your responsibility to clarify them for your subordinates. If you find that some under you do not work as hard and efficiently as they should, you must check whether the policies and goals of your division are, first, compatible with company policies, and second, set forth in such a way that they are understood by your employees.

5. Keep Out of the Way

I think the urge to work and be useful to others is a part of human nature. If you tell somebody, "Oh, you don't have to work. Go ahead and enjoy yourself," he or she will be delighted, but only for a while. Sooner or later, play for its own sake ceases to bring satisfaction. On the assumption that people have an inner drive to work, I discovered that one secret in getting employees to do their best was to let them get on with their work on their own. Consider the following: it is 8:30 A.M. and everyone is primed and eager to start. Then the boss comes in and preempts their morning by interjecting this order and that, and completely undermines their momentum and initiative. The boss's intention was to stir them to hard work, and it backfires. He might just as well have said, "Okay, let's take the day off," for the results will be the same.

I made a special effort throughout my career not to intervene where employees and staff were obviously hard at work. Of course, when something needed to be corrected or I could see a problem emerging, I was never silent, but I made a point of choosing my words and my timing in such a way as not to hinder the progress of the work.

When employees comment that a supervisor is "understanding" or "easy to work under," I interpret this to mean that the manager is the kind who lets his or her staff work without undue interference. All too often, however, managers are over-zealous in their shepherding and encouragement which, regardless of good intentions, is self-defeating. Letting people work without interference is to trust them, and we have to trust each other, even though no one can be expected to be 100 percent reliable. People do make mistakes, and you need to be alert to that, but my rule of thumb was that if I thought they were 60 percent trustworthy, I would leave the job up to them, while discretely monitoring their progress.

You will find that this policy is a useful guideline. It allows you to respect each subordinate's integrity and autonomy, and still lets you give advice and guidance at any time on major matters that come to your attention. My experience with this approach is that most of the time your expectations will be rewarded. If you want your employees to be both hard-working and enthusiastic, check yourself now and then to make sure you are giving them as much free rein as possible. Let them resolve the small matters but be ready to help with big problems.

6. Management for Conflict-Avoidance

Conflicts among employees or among management personnel can play havoc with the human relations within sections or departments of your company. Although not desirable, problems of this kind are bound to occur.

While some friction among employees has to be tolerated, as an experienced manager knows, a little extra care taken when making appointments can ease the situation considerably. If a department is run by three section chiefs, for example, there will be differences of opinion, especially if the three people have similar personalities and abilities. To prevent frequent confrontations, choose people who complement each other. Appoint one who is a good decision-maker, another skilled at mediating differences, and find a creative type for the third, for example. Together they will form an effective team that allows them to combine their distinctive talents without treading on each other's toes. Structuring such team management minimizes conflicts and helps immensely in running the department smoothly. Wise top management gives scrupulous attention to such considerations when making promotions and appointments.

Besides maintaining productive and smooth human interactions in your own department, you also have to think about incompatibility among the members of top management, of which you are one. Whatever you do to prevent disharmony is complicated by your being part of the group, but here, too, it is helpful to differentiate responsibilities and roles by skillful allocation of jobs.

When three managers are put together to form a team, for example, there may be problems if they are all of the same rank. This can be worked out by having one take final responsibility and getting the other two to agree to work in close consultation with that person. If you yourself take the lead, you will make the decisions yourself only after thorough discussion with the other two.

An old acquaintance of mine, a company president, once caused me great worry when he made a good friend of his the managing director of his company. I warned him of the risk he was taking in appointing a friend without the explicit proviso that their boss-lieutenant relationship take priority over their friendship. I wouldn't have been so concerned if he had established a clear understanding on that point, but without such an agreement their relationship as executives in the organization could be compromised. Suppose they failed to agree on some issue; their old bond as friends might get in the way of dealing with it properly, as president and managing director. The president might try to make a decision, only to meet resistance from the director. The resulting conflict would be complicated by their mutual inability to separate professional and personal loyalties. There should be no exceptions. Friction within management, as elsewhere in the company, can be avoided by creating the right combinations of personnel up and down the corporate hierarchy.

7. Coping with Failure

Sometimes we make mistakes that we did not foresee, and we fail at the task at hand. There are situations where we suddenly realize that we made the wrong decision, or something completely unforeseen occurs. It would be ideal if errors were never made, and although people do their best to avoid them, no one is omnipotent. It is unrealistic to expect flawless performance all the time.

What really matters is how mistakes are dealt with. The real gauge of character is in the way a person reacts when something goes wrong. The most constructive response is to humbly accept the blame and immediately set about correcting the situation. Some people, however, knowing they have made a mistake, plunge on, thinking only of saving face and convinced that there is "no turning back." Reacting that way often makes matters even worse, and it can cause more damage than the original mistake.

As the saying goes, "to err is human." We cannot expect to do everything perfectly 100 percent of the time; but when a mistake is made, it has to be corrected. People in top positions must be especially scrupulous about that. If a manager or executive tries to conceal what is clearly an error, the attempt at cover-up is likely to create even more trouble for the person in question and cause serious damage to the company and those connected with it. We need to be fully aware of the consequences of our own errors and demand of others as well as ourselves that they be rectified. At the same time, a good manager can forgive and forget the mistakes of others when honest efforts are made to put them right.

8. Commitment and Crisis

A company as a whole can usually run smoothly and grow steadily even though problems continually arise in different parts of the organization. Whether it is a corporation, a family, or even an individual, life rarely goes on year in and year out without some trouble or worry. This is one of the constants of being human.

What matters most is to be ready to face unpleasant challenges and to have solid principles and convictions with which to confront the problems we encounter. Whatever kind of work we do, we will face difficulties; how or if they can be resolved depends on our willingness to acknowledge them and our determination to overcome them. Without the courage to try, we are defenseless.

In my career I was very fortunate that we got through most crises with positive results. We might make a certain product and find that it simply did not sell. It was a downright failure. But the experience taught us lessons that later proved to be very valuable. On occasion we received indignant complaints from clients. A representative would come back with reports that a certain company was angry about this or that and would no longer do business with Matsushita Electric. When that happened, I never became discouraged. I saw it as an excellent opportunity to form an important bond between two corporations. My response was to tackle the problem head-on.

If I had been daunted by my own injured prestige and had backed off, making no attempt to defend my company or my convictions, the matter would have ended then and there in failure and embarrassment. But I considered our business to be something that transcended myself, an enterprise directed at the welfare of society and our customers. Because we constantly scrutinized our products and operations on the basis of that conviction, I was able to respond with confidence to criticism of the company.

Whatever the problem that had so provoked the customer, I believed it could always be remedied. I would tell the representative to go back and try to convey our corporate philosophy to the client. "Tell them you discussed the matter with me," I would say, "and then explain our thinking behind this product. Let them know that I do not believe it violates their business interests. The immediate problem may indeed involve shortcomings on our part, but our basic concern is to serve the needs and help the profitability of the customer. It would be unfortunate to reject our whole corporate philosophy because of one mistake. Try going through the whole thing again, and if they still don't want to have anything to do with us, gracefully withdraw. There's no need to worry or hesitate, just put it to them."

This kind of thing happened more than once. Usually the crisis was defused by persuasive explanation. The client would listen as our representative reviewed my ideas, and eventually would agree to reconsider the decision to stop doing business with Matsushita Electric. Many separate problems like that, once solved, provided the chance to form important and lasting ties with other companies.

9. Assessing Ability

From time to time, top management notices that a supervisor who was extremely able and hardworking as a rank-and-file employee has become listless and ineffective since being appointed to a more senior post. Similarly, a very capable and industrious section chief might produce an undistinguished record after promotion to department head.

Promotion by seniority is no longer the near-universal practice in Japanese industry it once was, but it is still the most common. That means that promotions are often made on the basis of considerations other than ability or merit. It may happen then that a person is initially elated in the promotion, but soon finds that the new job is more difficult than expected. Unable to meet its challenges, the recent appointee struggles in vain to fulfill the demands of the post, and ultimately the promotion does the company more harm than good.

Now if that person had an accurate perception of his own ability and realized that he was not capable of handling the job, he might have declined the offer saying, "I have confidence as section chief, but I do not think I have the ability to become department chief." Such a person would surely succeed in his job and be an effective section chief. Naturally it can also happen that, when a person with an unspectacular record is promoted on the basis of seniority, he or she turns out to have natural talent for the job.

In either case, we have to be accurate judges of our own abilities and seek work that uses our potential and fits within our limitations. On a scale of 100 points, if a person with an ability of, say, 50, attempts a job that requires 70, he or she will probably fail. A person with the ability of 100 who is assigned a job that demands only 70, on the other hand, may not fail, but would certainly be underused. The most productive match, for the individual and for society, is a job that challenges the worker but does not overwhelm.

It is especially important for people at the management level to be aware of their real abilities and seek out work that suits them. This is the secret to making employment enjoyable and fulfilling. As a company employee, or even as a human being, the most valuable achievements are not extraordinary deeds, but success in the tasks placed before you through conscientious and diligent effort.

We must remember, also, that ability and aptitude are not fixed or unchanging. Most people are constantly growing in their occupation. Many purposefully study or find other ways to acquire better qualifications and capabilities. It is important to be able to accurately gauge our abilities at any particular point in our careers and be careful not to take on jobs that exceed them, but at the same time we should constantly try to improve our capacities. The more skills and knowledge we acquire, the more ambitious projects and difficult assignments we can take on. A solid grasp of your own ability can magnify the enjoyment and satisfaction you receive from the labor you invest, including the confidence that you are making a significant contribution to society and the world.

10. Taking Charge

In an apt paraphrase, a friend once complained that there were "people, people everywhere, but no one to rely on." In business, there are usually any number of people available to do routine work but precious few who can rise to an emergency or unexpected development.

People who can take care of regular work are important, of course, and it is too much to expect that most of them would be capable of competently dealing with something extraordinary. But any company needs a number of employees who can quickly take charge when the going gets rough.

What makes an employee the kind who really makes a difference in a pinch? For one thing, a wealth of knowledge and experience, but that is not enough. What counts more is the constant readiness to lay one's career on the line to overcome difficult odds. Having people with these qualities can be the secret to a company's survival.

At one time, reading about Japan's phenomenal transformation into a modern state during the Meiji period (1868–1912), I was impressed by the account of a crisis in the government. As the situation deteriorated, the cabinet members recognized what was happening and started submitting their resignations. At this point the Meiji emperor is said to have observed, "It is all very well for you to resign and back out, but what am I to do? I cannot resign." In 1868, the emperor was reinstated as sovereign ruler after a period of several centuries during which the court had not exercised real power. The government became a constitutional monarchy with Emperor Meiji as the authority of last resort. Indeed, he could not resign.

To me, his words echoed the resoluteness with which he met and managed each crisis, regardless of the risk to himself and the newly reinvigorated imperial institution. In fact, from a culturally remote, industrially backward country without trains, telecommunications, or machines, and despite tremendous handicaps, Japan made itself into one of the five strongest powers in the world in a matter of forty-five years. Without the leadership of this indefatigable ruler during a time of relentless change, such a feat would not have been possible. Management personnel today face challenges of a considerably smaller scale, but they too need to be always prepared for crisis in the course of day-to-day work, as Emperor Meiji was in creating the modern state. The capacity to move boldly when the situation demands is as vital for a company as it is in running a nation.

11. Worth the Worry

A day at the office for a company manager or executive is never without a stream of problems. Although the work may look as though it were proceeding smoothly in the department or factory, the person in charge typically feels harassed, as one matter after another presses for a resolution. At times there is so much to attend to that the worry-ridden manager cannot even sleep or eat with peace of mind. Many carry on with a kind of desperation, their attention riveted to the search for solutions that they hope, someday, will bring some peace and quiet in which to work.

I do not believe, actually, that a person with ambition in business ever attains tranquility or peace of mind. All one can do is to keep on pushing, slowly but steadily, toward that goal. Thinking back over the early years of my own career, each day was a battle, a struggle for survival. We worked with the dreaded thought in the back of our minds that if we made one serious mistake, the whole enterprise might cave in. There were very few nights when I could sleep soundly without thoughts of unfinished business running through my head.

Yet the painstaking toil we engage in and its entourage of worry and anxiety are intrinsic to the nature of work. Precisely because we meet and conquer each oncoming dilemma, do we achieve a degree of success and build our business today into something greater than it was yesterday.

It is the same with any endeavor—like government. A country's leaders invest heart and soul into the development of their nation despite constant threats from within and without. At the same time, the international environment evolves and the country's status within it changes. Today the United States, leader of the world throughout the postwar decades, has lost its dominance and with it much of its former power. Its decline is a measure of the vicissitudes of the times, which wrench nations out of the grasp even of the most dedicated, courageous, and hardworking leaders.

The ups and downs in our companies, our departments, and the individuals who work within them, are even more violent. It is no wonder that worries and troubles are an inherent part of the business routine. Work would not be work without them.

Painful and complex as our business endeavors may be, I believe we can find meaning in them as we grapple with anxiety. First we must accept the fact that worry and uncertainty are part and parcel of a manager's vocation; if it becomes intolerable, there is no choice but to resign.

For the seasoned manager, however, every difficulty, every challenge should be considered a chance to learn, a stimulus to produce something better and more innovative. Those experiences may be bitter, but each time we overcome the odds we are given new opportunities to do better. I truly believe that here is where one can find the real fulfillment and satisfaction that a job in management provides.

12. Believe in the Possible

In business today, all manner of new methods are being developed, in production and technology, sales, and related fields. The pace of change seems astounding to us now, but when we think about it, what is progress from a contemporary point of view will be antiquated in 100 years. Our descendants will look at our "revolutionary" and "state-of-the-art" technology and smile at how unsophisticated it is. That is the nature of progress in human civilization.

In 100 years, much of what we now believe to be out of the question is likely to be possible. Of course, bigger, more awesome problems will emerge as well, and human beings, as long as they survive on earth, will go on unraveling the secrets of science and discovering new technologies and more advanced arts. I believe that people in industry, particularly those in management, can get a clear vision of their mission and role in society only in the context of the infinite resources of human invention.

If we believe firmly enough in the wide horizon of our potential, any endeavor we undertake will eventually be successful. It may turn out to be excruciatingly difficult, but its successful completion, grounded in the conviction that anything is possible, will look easy to an observer. You must always remember that no matter how difficult the task, there is always a better way to do it, and hold the belief that whatever you set out to do, you can and will, somehow, accomplish.

In business, those in leadership positions have to believe that. Once you have a goal that you believe can be attained or an original concept you are certain can be developed, you gather your subordinates and forcefully put your case to them: "Now here's what we want to do. Will you give it a try? I know you can do it, and I want you to give it your best. If you'll work together on this project, I will take the lead and shoulder the responsibility." If you are persuasive enough, your employees will throw all their weight behind you and willingly take on the project. Most of the time they will succeed.

It is necessary, of course, that your project or objective be reasonable and feasible; if so, you can be confident that it will be carried out according to plan, regardless of unforeseen difficulties arising along the way. I adopted this kind of approach in my own business, and I found that if a responsible manager appeals to employees with energy and conviction, their knowledge and skills coalesce naturally into a reservoir of shared know-how. Their combined capabilities produce new discoveries and more innovative, better methods, in production and technology, sales techniques, and even management procedures.

Personnel in positions of responsibility, therefore, cannot afford to be passive or pessimistic. They cannot be deterred by difficulty or expect failure before success. They have to have the aggressive persistence that enables them to accomplish what they set out to do. If they stumble or fall, they get up and stand more solidly than before as they drive toward fulfillment of their goal. These qualities are absolutely essential to a manager in business today.

13. Attachment Grows

It may be easier to apply the various principles and ideas offered in the foregoing pages if you consider one further point. Everyone in business, from newly hired recruits to veteran managers, should think very carefully about this, the central dimension of your involvement in the company: You have to love your work genuinely and deeply. It sounds so simple and ordinary, but it is very important.

If you do a job only because you have been requested to by your employer, you will not do it well. The activity takes on a completely different meaning if you find your work engaging. In the midst of a particularly difficult assignment, you may find your friends feeling sorry for you. Indeed, job-related matters will keep you awake nights, make your spouse uneasy, and cause your acquaintances to worry about your health. But while your situation may appear miserable to others, you are not suffering at all. To be totally absorbed in a challenge and thinking about it all the time is not a chore but a pleasure.

The optimism and resilience to overcome obstacles depends on whether or not you like your work. If you supervise other employees, you must work with all kinds of people. Some argue at every turn, others consistently misunderstand you, and still others seem unable to consider your ideas with an open mind. This can be depressing, irritating, and frustrating. Even then, you do not give in, but continue to believe that there is a way of getting through to a slow-witted subordinate and helping him to do a good job. You never stop trying to persuade the stubborn worker to cooperate.

If you like your job, it will never feel onerous to you. Troublesome problems and hard dilemmas will not shake your confidence; you know you can overcome them and later enjoy what you have accomplished. Those moments strengthen the courage with which you undertake your work. If you dislike what you are doing, nothing goes well. You become more miserable and probably develop chronic headaches. If your fondest dream is to give up and quit as soon as you can, you will not be able to finish any jobs you have started.

Every field holds such perils for the uncommitted. You will be an outstanding painter only if you like to paint; someone who doesn't like art will never become an artist, no matter how hard he or she tries. It is hard enough to excel in art even if you truly like it. Success is all the more elusive for one whose heart is not really in the work.

People committed to a career in business owe it to themselves, their colleagues, and their company to understand the secrets of success. That is basic know-how, without which we struggle and fulfillment evades us, no matter how assiduously we apply ourselves. It is an almost intuitive proficiency that one absorbs through personal experience and spontaneous self-discovery; it is not something that can be taught. What others tell you may become useful information, but the knack of being a talented professional is ultimately built up as you discover yourself through accumulated experience. You probably have to put up with harsh words, rapped knuckles, and humiliating treatment from your seniors, but the buffeting of these experiences will sharpen your skills and increase your knowledge.

Anyone who survives in a company career to that point has to like their work. Otherwise, the learning process would bring only frustration and perplexity rather than new insights into the way your profession works best.

84

The most basic of the precepts presented in this volume about how to pursue a successful career in business is that: you have to like your work. Ask yourself whether you really like your job. Perhaps the answer is "no," in which case it pays to make a deliberate effort to develop an interest in it. If you try, it is possible to recast the image of unrewarding struggle into a new perception of an occupation you enjoy immensely. The way you approach your work—your attitude and perspective— strongly influences the quality of performance by those around you, as well. Work ought to be so engaging that you do not tire. A hobby or two is a good diversion, but it should not take up other time needed for further study. If you can balance an absorbing job, useful study, and necessary relaxation, you will become a valuable employee, and more, you will find that your work is a real blessing.

PART TWO
Thoughts on Life

Preface

As OF THIS writing I am nearing my ninetieth birthday. Even today, however, I can clearly remember the day at the age of nine when I stood on the platform of the country station of Kinokawa to say goodbye to my mother and take up an apprenticeship in the faraway city of Osaka. The intervening 81 years have been most eventful. Some think I must have had a hard life, but oddly enough I never feel that way at all. I simply worked hard, absorbing myself in my work, from one day to the next. Through the years I have seen dramatic change, faced some memorable challenges, and met many fascinating people, all of which have made me what I am today. Recalling it all, I am filled with a feeling of gratitude for all I have learned from the world around me, from the wisdom of others, and from the work I have pursued.

From time to time I have in the past been asked to share my reflections on my experiences with others, and I have always been glad to do so. This volume brings together a selection of these reflections centering on the general topic of life.

Life is endlessly complex, difficult to explain, and full of inexhaustible mystery. Since even at this advanced age, I have a great deal yet to learn, I do not presume to lecture others in this book about how to live. I simply hope that by sharing these accounts and thoughts from my experience, readers may be able to better guide their own lives and activities.

KONOSUKE MATSUSHITA
August 1983

1. Navigating Life

Success is possible in any endeavor that respects the laws of nature. Before you act, first ask yourself honestly whether your project will violate those laws.

Think for a moment what it is to make an ocean voyage. As you move out into the boundless, sometimes tumultuous expanses, your progress is peaceful and smooth at times, and at other times you are tossed by rough waters and buffeted by heavy gales. You may lose your bearings and your vessel may be damaged or wrecked, leaving you adrift, pitiless and lost.

Ocean travel today is much safer and more pleasant than it used to be, thanks to advances in navigation and shipbuilding technology. We owe those achievements to the wisdom that placed priority on discovering how to work within the laws of nature to ensure the safest, speediest journey. The forces of nature reign supreme in the ocean. Strong winds course over it, whipping up the waters, and as the waves rise, your ship rolls. It would be foolhardy and dangerous to try and keep your ship from rolling despite the waves. You would have to force the equipment to perform in ways that were beyond its capacities and this would lead to disaster. You can't defy the laws of the nature.

In the voyage of life, the same rule applies. How does one learn how to live in accordance with the laws of nature? It is not particularly difficult. All you have to do is act with your instincts and follow tried and true wisdom and good sense. When it rains, put up an umbrella. When you feel ill and feverish, stop to rest and recuperate. When people help you, thank them sincerely. If you are a manufacturer, make good quality products, sell them at a reasonable price, and scrupulously settle your accounts. When business is poor, be patient; instead of forcing sales even at the expense of profit, wait until they begin to sell again at your price, and then go back to full-scale production.

These are natural rules. If we follow them, we will enjoy good health, get along with others, and our professional endeavors will flourish. All goes well as long as we observe nature's laws. If, however, we become so preoccupied with an idea that we neglect nature's injunctions, frustration and defeat invariably overwhelm us. Napoleon is famous for the arrogant remark that the word "impossible" did not exist in his dictionary. Now, clearly many things are beyond human control, like the process of growing old or, eventually, dying. Look at what happened to Napoleon himself at the end. He was banished to the island of St. Helena and died in misery and unhappiness. So on one interpretation Napoleon's claim seems presumptuous and absurd, for it ignores basic human limitations.

From another perspective, however, it has the ring of truth. Things which violate the laws of nature are indeed impossible. Eternal youth, for instance, is an eternal pipe dream— people age whether they want to or not. Yet, the spirit of humankind is such that the reverse is also true: whatever is consonant with the laws of nature is possible, whether it concerns one's health, or interpersonal relations, or the conduct of one's business. Thus Napoleon's dictum does indeed express an important truth about human potential but in the end he succumbed to the temptation to go beyond this and flaunt nature itself. In doing so, he sowed the seeds of his own destruction. Life's journey may be tumultuous, but if we face its challenges openly and without prejudice, and strive to learn what is right and sensible, there will always be a way to surmount them.

2. Maximize Your Destiny

Do your best and leave the rest up to Heaven.
Whether you make the most of your destiny depends
on how you live your life.

Looking back over my life I cannot help noticing the large role destiny played in the way it unfolded. Why did I go into the manufacture and sales of electric appliances? Why was I able to build a tiny workshop into a multinational corporation? Many factors came into play, but in the final analysis I can only say that what I achieved was very much determined by fate, the luck of the draw.

Certainly at each crucial juncture, I did my utmost, and I managed to avoid major setbacks while one success led to another. But by any standards, my efforts were not extraordinary. I was surrounded by people far more able, better educated, and physically stronger than me, and yet my efforts in business were blessed with success beyond my wildest dreams. Destiny is the only way I can explain it.

Perhaps one of my strengths was to fully exploit, although unconsciously, what fortune seemed to bring my way. At the age of nine, poverty forced me to live away from my family and become a shop apprentice. I took advantage of that chance to receive training in a commercial trade, an experience that taught me discipline and strengthened me through hardship. Since I had a weak constitution, it was especially important that I earn goodwill and help from my co-workers. I had only a few years of formal education, and so I tried to compensate by seeking out advice from others. Then, more than once there were accidents when I narrowly escaped death, which only made me more certain that luck was on my side. Intuitively, I saw promise in every turn of my fate, and I made constructive use of it. I believe that is why the path before me was always open.

Fate represents a power beyond human control, to be sure—we have no control over the circumstances of our birth, our physical constitution or our mental acuity. But that does not mean that we have absolutely no control over our lives. Indeed, the possibility of human intervention creates the mystique and fascination of fate. By your attitude and actions, you may be able to influence the way fate manifests itself. The wise old saying, "Do your best and leave the rest to Heaven," seems to tell us just that. Whether you take full advantage of your destiny depends very much on how you live your life in all its aspects: you can help determine your lifespan by taking good care of your health; you can enhance your inherent abilities by study and training.

How much margin do we have to shape our own destinies? I am not sure how appropriate it is to try to express this numerically, but my own observations suggest that human effort accounts for only about 10 to 20 percent. But that small portion has an effect on how the 80 or 90 percent determined by fate, and in fact determines whether your fate is radiant or lusterless.

Common sense tells us that we ought to do everything within our power to enhance that 10-20 percent, treading the path of life with faith and conviction. Knowing the limits of our own powers, we do not grow conceited when a major success comes our way, nor do we become disheartened when we encounter failure. I believe that anyone who strides confidently and honestly along their self-chosen path will be treated well by destiny.

3. The Gem of Human Nature

At the core of human nature is a diamond in the rough that promises to radiate brilliance, but it will shine only if you keep polishing it.

Our understanding of what it means to be human is basic to our views on interpersonal relations and how people should live. We interact with others and live our lives in various ways, all depending on our perception of humankind. The meaning of "human" has been characterized in many different ways. Some see people from the perspective of intellect, others from a religious point of view, and yet others in the more concrete terms of daily experience. Human beings appear strong to some, weak to others. They are called "intellectual animals," "social animals," and are sometimes seen as having transcendent elements of sanctity or buddhahood within them. In still another view, to be human is to be ordinary, mortal, always straying from the path of virtue, and filled with avarice. Perhaps all of these labels are accurate, but during my lifetime I have come to believe that whatever else they may be, at base people have an inborn greatness.

My health was never robust, and even after I set up shop on my own as a manufacturer of electric appliances, I often had to leave the factory and rest in bed for a while. Physically unable to perform all the jobs expected of the chief, I had no alternative but to entrust much of my work to reliable people working under me. I didn't do it halfway. I gave them full responsibility for certain areas, telling them, "Come and consult me only about the most crucial matters. Otherwise, manage things as you think best." Proud to be trusted so completely, this corps of able and loyal managers were inspired to extraordinary efforts. Their main thought was, "My boss needs me now, and has given me an important job. He is ill, and I'm going to give it everything I've got." They were able to give full play to their abilities, and their enthusiasm was infectious. Working together with their colleagues toward set goals, they created tremendously effective teams. For them, one plus one made four. This gave us a strong advantage that allowed our company to undertake especially large projects from time to time.

My personal experience gradually convinced me that human beings are indeed magnificent, capable of unlimited achievements, given the chance. The core of human nature is like an uncut diamond. It has the innate property of brilliance, but it will not shine without cutting and polishing. Everyone has within them wisdom, ability, and other qualities as precious as diamonds. One's abilities may at first appear unlikely to produce even a little gleam, but if they are properly polished, they will be radiant. We need to realize this, and strive individually and together to fulfill the potential we have. If we do, our inherent qualities will glow.

In fact, we owe it to ourselves and our societies to open our eyes to our own noble qualities and have confidence in them. Expand and refine them, as if you were polishing a diamond, and make yourself into what you can and should be. The effects of that effort will be incalculable. The world would be a better place if all people believed in their inner greatness and worked hard to let it shine. We would no longer regard

human beings as weak, untrustworthy, selfish, and con-
tentious. That attitude, which certainly contributes to the
suffering we create, would be overwhelmed by our awareness
of wonderful human qualities, and we would create instead
prosperity, peace, and happiness.

4. Success as a Person

Use your natural gifts to the maximum. Live your life in fulfillment of yourself and others, for that is where you will find the path to success.

I think everyone wants to be successful in life. Many are taught from childhood how important it is to be successful, and they genuinely believe that whatever the cost, they must succeed in life. Others learn to value success later. But what is a successful life?

We generally measure success by social status, prestige, wealth, or all three. In business, people who are considered successful are those whose enterprises grow, creating bigger profits, expanded assets, and greater renown for the entrepreneur. That is certainly one kind of success, but I believe there must be another, even more significant measure of success as well.

There is an old adage, "Ten men, ten minds." Everyone is different from everyone else, as we are all born with particular dispositions and abilities. No two people have exactly the same character, temperament, or talents. The fact that we are all different means that we are predestined for different avocations and lifestyles. Some have gifts for and a sense of mission in politics, some in scholarly pursuits, while others have natural abilities as doctors, technicians, painters, singers, architects, accountants, shopkeepers, and so forth.

The second kind of success comes from making the most of your natural gifts, regardless of what they are, and fulfilling a role that you feel is so much part of you that it becomes a mission. I believe that living in pursuit of such goals and achieving them is what success in life really means. It is the way we are meant to live. For some, therefore, success lies in carrying out the work of a Cabinet minister, or becoming a shoemaker who is happy when his customers are pleased with their shoes. The yardstick for success is not social status, prestige, or size of bank account, but how well your endeavors are matched with your natural gifts and mission, and how fully your gifts are employed.

Viewed in the narrow terms of status and money, success can be a perilous objective. To achieve those things, your efforts will be frantic and unnatural, probably distorting or even eroding your innate abilities and character. If your natural inclinations lie elsewhere, perhaps you will find the goals you have set for yourself to be unexpectedly hard to obtain, which can lead to deep disappointment and a sense of inferiority. Some people in this situation lose all interest in life itself. It is better to remember that not everyone can or should become a company president or respected Cabinet minister, nor can everyone be extremely wealthy.

It is possible for anyone, however, if we have the right attitude, to live in fulfillment of our natural endowments. Those who do live that way experience pride and confidence to the full, and lead active lives, regardless of wealth or social position. The more such people a society has, the more vital and dynamic it will be.

Recently there is a rising tide of restlessness and discontent even though we have more material comforts in our lives than ever before. I cannot help but connect such dissatisfaction with the way people look at success. Generally, so much emphasis is placed on social status, prestige, and money as the measure of a person, that we tend to forget the value in using our natural endowments and dedicating our lives to the mission we were born to fulfill. This tendency can be seen even in companies, schools, and other organizations. Success of that kind is elusive; its pursuit can only breed dissatisfaction.

Success in life, success as a human being, is the fruit of your efforts to fully use your natural gifts. Honest efforts to fulfill your potential will leave no room for discontent, but will, rather, enhance your joy in life, and the social benefits of a contented populace will be just as great.

5. Finding Your Natural Talents

To discover your natural talents, first you need a strong desire to know what they are. Hold on to that desire, and in the course of your day-to-day life, you will find them.

If you want to be successful as a person, first and foremost you must know what your inborn abilities and characteristics are. Otherwise you will not know how to fully use them. Still, that is easier said than done. It is difficult sometimes to know what we are suited for, because our talents are by no means always obvious. But a little mystery adds to the spice of life; the process itself of finding your strengths can add a lot of interest and depth to everything you do.

But the desire to discover your natural abilities comes first. If that desire remains strong, you will always be alert and ready to recognize those talents in the course of daily life. A small voice inside, for example, might tell you at some point which direction to take. Or in the context of a minor incident or event, you might discover that you have an aptitude in a totally unexpected area. In some cases, other people will point out to you an aptitude or talent you were unaware of. If you want to know what those talents are, you will recognize them either by yourself or when someone else suggests them to you. If you don't care, even the loudest of hints will pass right by.

103

It is also essential to keep an open mind. An untrapped mind is selfless, able to see things as they really are and make good judgments. Preoccupation, bias, preconceptions are traps, inducing you into taking too much credit, for example, or distorting sound advice, so that you set out on endeavors that are not suited to you at all.

Children also need to be shown how to see themselves and the world around them with untrapped minds. It is important to create the kind of home and school environments that let children explore and help them find their own talents. A creative, productive society as a whole, in fact, is one that helps people to discover their natural gifts by providing an environment that makes it easy to find them.

If each one of us tries hard to discover and use the abilities we were born with, we make the way easier for everyone to find success and happiness. More, if we all work to fulfill a role that is naturally suited to our innate abilities, we will never find ourselves caught in a forced, impossible endeavor or wasteful competition. The whole society will function smoothly, becoming a base for real prosperity.

6. Trust Comes First

A person who is trusted responds by trying hard to meet your expectations. Trust others completely, even if you know your trust might be betrayed.

In my long career, I have worked with many people, and I have had business and other relationships with all kinds. What I feel most keenly as I look back now is how extraordinary people are and how magnificently they respond to your trust in them. They almost always come through. I have also found that mutual trust helps everyone, materially and spiritually, and creates good relationships.

In 1917 when I started my own business manufacturing electric fixtures, the only employees were my wife Mumeno and her younger brother Toshio Iue (founder of Sanyo Electric Co., Ltd.). It was not long before the demand for our products was too much for the three of us to handle, and so we hired our first non-family employees. With four or five new faces, an unexpected problem arose. In those days we made light-bulb sockets and attachment plugs. The sockets contained an insulation material that we had invented. This material, consisting of asphalt, asbestos, and powdered stone, was an innovation in a new field. The problem was whether I should let our new workers know how the insulation was manufactured. All companies producing this kind of material kept their technical know-how a closely guarded secret, known only to the family members and relatives involved in making it.

I thought a lot about it. If I kept the method a tight secret as other factories did, then my wife and her brother would have to handle that entire area of production themselves. We also would have to keep the other employees away from the insulation production area, which would be inefficient and troublesome. What worried me even more, however, was the attitude toward my employees that this implied. Was it right to leave them out, when they were our colleagues working together with us? I finally decided that all our workers had an equal right to know the manufacturing process, and so I taught them how to make the insulation and put them in charge of it.

A fellow electric fixtures maker warned me that letting new employees know our technique risked leaking our know-how to others. If that happened, not only our enterprise but all others in the field would face stiffer competition. I thanked him for his advice, but I firmly believed that would not happen. If you trust your workers, they will not betray you by leaking secrets.

My faith in them was justified. No one ever talked about the technique outside the factory. More important, the fact that I had entrusted them with confidential manufacturing processes boosted their morale and helped immeasurably to create an atmosphere at the factory where everyone felt needed and welcomed, and the result was better performance.

From then on, I trusted my employees and gave them important tasks as much as possible. For example, I asked one young man of only twenty to undertake the significant job of opening an office in Kanazawa. I also left product development to my most reliable employees. In these and other cases, they almost always performed better than I had expected.

From these experiences, I learned early on the importance of mutual trust. If I had not trusted my employees, I would have caused disappointment and pain for all of us, not to speak of the inefficiency that would have resulted. People all feel love, hate, and other emotions, and the average person usually is careful to calculate his own gain or loss. But it is dangerous to get too enmeshed in emotions and calculations of personal gain, for once you do, you become suspicious of everyone, assuming that all they want is to get what you have or to push you down. That is distrust, and it produces nothing but unhappiness, inefficiency, and disloyalty.

Trust people. Now and then you may end up being cheated or having to sustain a loss, but do not be discouraged. If you can sustain your trust in people so much that not even the occasional betrayal can break it, the person who would still try to deceive you would be rare indeed. I truly believe that virtually no one would try to deceive someone who really trusts them.

7. A Thankful Heart

> *We must never forget to feel gratitude. People with a thankful heart treat others with consideration, treasure the things around them, and find real joy in living.*

A long time ago, perhaps partly because I wasn't in very good health, I went through a period of gloom and constant mental fatigue. One day I ran into a close friend, who gave me some very sound advice when I confided my melancholy mood. "I don't know why," I told him, "but these days I've been feeling very low. I get lonely and pessimistic about life."

Right away he responded, "You are experiencing a kind of depression." That took me aback, but as I thought about it, it made sense to me. "You're probably right, but what do you think is the cause?" I asked him. "It's quite simple," he said, and explained in the following way.

"You probably feel no joy at anything, and don't appreciate the value of the things right around you. From my point of view, you are in an enviable situation, but you don't seem to have any idea how lucky you are. You have so much that makes your life possible, like all the air you need right at your fingertips, but you don't seem grateful at all. Of course you feel desolate. If you appreciate those things that keep you alive, the world will become a very pleasant place. You will tackle each distasteful problem as it arises without letting it bother you."

That made me think hard. Once in a while I had reflected how good my circumstances were, but I had not truly appreciated everything I had. Certainly I never stopped to consider that I had all the air I needed to keep on living! My company and my mission through work were important, I thought, but without air for five minutes I would be left helpless and would die. Instead of being thankful for the limitless abundance of air, that essential ingredient for life, I had been preoccupied and depressed by the unceasing flow of immediate problems in the company. I could see now that I was on the wrong track.

Taking a new perspective, I realized how fruitless it is to agonize over trifles. I knew that I should focus my energy on much more important things from then on.

We are blessed with air, water, the sun, and all else that nature provides us. Not only that, every day of our lives we have parents, brothers, sisters, colleagues, friends, and many others who help us go on. We all have a family heritage, ancestors, a country, and so much more.

Yet we take them for granted, despite the fact that they are so very important to us. That is why discontent can creep into our lives, deepening until it becomes depression. In short, we make our lives dreary and desolate all by ourselves.

When you express the gratitude you feel for all those essential things you have, people might think how odd you are. They are too wrapped up in their affairs to care, but no one should ever be too busy to consider with gratitude how much we are given. Gratitude is important. It infuses you with humility and the will to care about the little things. It inspires you to find joy in life, to leave your tensions behind, and to respect others. You will find that the little quarrels and conflicts no longer crop up. Whenever you feel distracted by worry or anger, remind yourself how grateful you are for all you have.

8. Know What to Fear

To be completely fearless can be very dangerous.
Be aware of what threatens you, for that knowledge
can save you from precipitous or unwise acts.

We can lead more focused lives by knowing what to be afraid of and when. Some people believe that only cowards show fear and that a coward accomplishes nothing, but I am not talking about timidity. Rather, by fear I mean deep respect and humility in the face of what is stronger than we are. In that sense, children ought to have a healthy measure of fear for their parents or teachers; salespersons ought to be afraid of the proprietor; employees, their president. Even a company president should have some fear of the public and the consumer. Moreover, it is wise to be wary not only of others, but of yourself also. If you tend to be lazy, arrogant, or lack the courage and conviction to accomplish what you set out to do, you need to watch yourself.

What I am speaking here is not the fear of danger to life and limb—such as being bitten by a dog. Rather it is the human and social forces acting on us and in us that we must hold in awe. If we do not , we will inadvertently become self-centered, naive, or arrogant, inviting our own self destruction. Fearing nothing, Adolf Hitler grew confident all out of proportion, leading him to wield power indiscriminately until he destroyed himself. This is why I say that nothing is more dangerous than fearlessness.

In everything we do, we should always be aware of that danger—even to the point of deliberately seeking out the sources of our fear. A modicum of fear sustains the modesty and prudence needed to get along smoothly in life. It helps us to map out our actions cautiously and to judge accurately the wisest path to take. A measure of fear often helps us to choose well among options and pushes us to develop our strengths and potential.

The same point can be made with respect to a company or other type of organization—even governments. An organization or government that does not fear anything or anyone inevitably overestimates its own strength and often resorts to coercion and abuse of power. Whatever glory it may earn will be only brief, for its arrogance will inevitably lead to its decline. History is filled with examples. While the individual has to be wary of rash behavior born of over-confidence, people who form organizations must be all the more careful not to allow the kind of hubris that creates a "tyranny of the majority." It seems to me that a fundamental problem in the world today is a dangerous overconfidence that is bred by too little fear.

9. Human Feelings Count

> *Human emotions do not always follow the dictates of reason. As we build relationships, words and deeds should take into account the subtle factors that affect the feelings of others.*

It is a mystery of the human heart, but even the most trivial things can cause jubilance, sadness, or indignation; they can raise our hopes or dash us into despair. In order for people to function successfully together and do well as a community, corporation, nation, or any other group, they have to be aware of human feelings. The same is true in anything you attempt.

Let me illustrate with an episode concerning the way an income tax was introduced by the newly-founded Meiji government (1868–1912). Having been summoned by the local tax office, a group of prominent and wealthy citizens of the city of Osaka were gathered in the posh banquet hall of Tomitaya, a first-class traditional restaurant. In those days the government was very powerful, not to be questioned, and so they sat stiffly in the tatami-matted room wondering nervously what the occasion was all about.

A man entered, who was obviously the head of the local tax office. Instead of proceeding to the front of the room, however, he went to the lowest-ranking seat at the back, discreetly indicating his deference to the assembled guests. From this humble position and in very polite language he explained that a new tax was to be assessed on their incomes; he hoped they would give their full cooperation. Then, as an expression of the government's goodwill, he invited them to enjoy the food and drink served.

In the Meiji era there was a strong tendency for the government to act arbitrarily, without considering the feelings of ordinary people. The tax office could simply have issued a notice announcing the new tax or called the leading citizens to the office, but the Osaka tax office chief chose a very different tack. Instead of issuing orders he treated the community leaders with utmost courtesy. By explaining the new system in clear, polite language and asking for their support in making it work, he showed genuine consideration for the feelings of the taxpayers.

This kind of scrupulous consideration for others is necessary every day of our lives. People have many reasons for their acts. Consideration for personal gain or loss is sometimes paramount, sometimes irrelevant. In making a request, if a person is arrogant or high-handed, he or she may be refused no matter how generous the remuneration. On the other hand, a request made with sincerity and respect will often get a good response even if it entails some loss. What we do so often depends on feelings and reactions that may not always be clear and rational.

When you ask someone a favor, therefore, you should be aware that your attitude can determine the response. By paying attention to the delicate sensitivities of others, we can cultivate better relations with them. It is a good idea, therefore, to stop now and then and consciously think about whether we are tuned to other people's feelings and whether our behavior reflects our consideration.

10. The Lessons of Daily Life

> *Big successes or failures are not the only experiences from which we can learn. Even the most ordinary events of daily life and work can be very instructive if you are willing to learn from them.*

Seeing something once is worth more than hearing about it one hundred times, as the old saying goes. Still, no matter how many times we see something, often we do not really understand it without testing it for ourselves. Take something like salt. It is white and crystalline, but you can gaze at a pile of salt for hours and use every trick of your imagination without grasping that essential quality of salt—its taste. One sample on your tongue is enough to tell you exactly what salt tastes like. In short, you may not understand the true nature of something until you directly experience it.

Older people are respected partly because of the experience they have accumulated. Their perceptivity and judgment are greater and more reliable than those of their juniors. Without much experience, a person cannot lay any real claim to seniority.

How does one gain experience? Significant achievements and failures, of course, drive lessons home with special impact, but you can also acquire deep insight from ordinary, everyday life if you just keep your attention focused on what it teaches. In fact, the lessons learned from routine experience may be the most important of all.

For example, in the course of your daily work, even when you are satisfied with a job, you may see how you could have done it even better. Reflect carefully on what you have done and you can learn from it. Work consists of little successes and little failures. If you pay close attention to them, they offer valuable hints that can enhance your work and life.

Minor experiences embedded quietly in an apparently routine daily life can be as valuable to you as your more memorable successes or failures. It seems to me that the accumulation of such ordinary lessons of living are especially important today, to help us cope with the dizzying pace of change around us.

11. Treasure Both Strengths and Weaknesses

Don't let your strengths go to your head; don't feel inferior for your shortcomings. They are both part of your distinctive individuality.

People are not gods. No one is perfect, knows everything, and can do everything. We all have strong points and failings, a unique set for each one of us. People usually take pride in one and regret the other, feeling either superior or inferior to others as the case may be. But do our individual strengths and weaknesses really warrant either kind of reaction? Are they so easy to pin down in the first place?

All of us have encountered situations in which merits can become demerits, and vice versa. This is certainly true of most of my acquaintances in business. I have known many in management who combine knowledge, eloquence, and dynamism—just the sort of gifted all-rounders one would expect to lead their companies to great success. The reality does not always work that way, however; more often than not it is the ordinary person, an executive with no particularly striking talents, whose company forges ahead in leaps and bounds.

This phenomenon is possible because of the transformation, in certain situations, of strengths into weaknesses and weaknesses into strengths. In a company environment, managers whose knowledge and skills enable them to do any task on their own tend not to consult their colleagues or staff for either help or opinions. Some dismiss well-meant suggestions with a curt, "I already know that." Eventually the staff stop offering opinions and just stick to what they've been told to do. Even when they actually do entrust someone else with a given task, such managers tend to poke their noses into every detail of its execution. These people kill their employees' potential for initiative and hinder exchange of ideas within the organization. In that sense, they stand in the way of the company's growth.

Managers with average personal talents, on the other hand, may have the opposite effect. They do not try to take on everything themselves but instead ask their staff for suggestions and delegate responsibility. This sparks their employees' enthusiasm and helps create an open forum for ideas and opinions. The resulting collective effort drives the company to greater and greater success.

The inversion of people's strengths and weaknesses occurs in all areas of our lives, and suggests that we need not make such a fuss about either. Both are natural endowments contributing to each person's unique personality. In specific situations they emerge as either good points or bad points; but in the broader picture of things, they exist, like the faces we each bear, neither good nor detrimental, not right or wrong.

It is natural that we take pride in our strengths and feel shame about our weaknesses. We should, moreover, try to build up our natural gifts and correct our failings. But it is far more important to avoid being overconcerned about our strength-weakness balance sheet and get on with making the most of the uniqueness we each possess.

12. Ask, Then Listen Carefully

When in trouble, ask for advice. Know yourself well, and weigh the advice of others in good faith. These are the foundations of a secure life.

No one escapes the various dilemmas that crop up in life. At work, we may worry about how we should approach a new job, or wonder whether we are really suited to the one we have. In our private lives, we fret about things like marriage and the choices that affect our future. From major decisions that will have an impact on our whole life to the most mundane choices, life is full of moments when we ask ourselves, "What should I do?"

Often we just make our own choices there and then, but sometimes we get stuck, unable to pick an alternative. At such times, the advice of others is often invaluable. Friends, family, teachers, supervisors—people who know us well will often provide, when asked, a perfect solution. I have always sought the opinion of others when I can't decide alone what to do. Right from the day I started our family business with my wife and her brother, until this very day, I have been in many situations where decisions seemed too tough to handle on my own, such as whether I should take on a new business venture. For me, it has always been extremely valuable to explain the problem to another person and ask, "What do you think I should do?"

Some people I turned to would try to talk me out of a plan, others would urge me to go for it, and still others would caution me that the time was not quite right. If they convinced me, I would go right ahead and act accordingly. If I was still wavering, I would simply get another perspective by asking someone else. In the end, after considering a range of views, I made my own decision. I speak only from my own experience, but a surprising number of people responded to my requests for advice by saying something like, "I'm glad you asked me about that. I've been thinking for some time now that you should probably do such-and-such." After all this time, I am thoroughly convinced that one should never hesitate to seek the counsel of others.

When seeking the opinions of others, however, it is important to have a strong sense of your own identity. It lets you listen from a positive, yet critical position. Otherwise, all the opinions you hear will sound correct, and you will find yourself tossed from this view to that each time you ask. At the other extreme, if you are too wrapped up in yourself, or concerned only to further your own interests, you will hear only what you want to hear, in which case there is no real point in asking at all. There are as many routes to any destination as there are people trying to get there, and it is no use trying to get there by any way other than that which your own unique nature guides you. Therefore, whether ideas come from people, books, or even television, weigh your options honestly, based on a firm and dispassionate self-understanding.

The judgment and resources of just one person are limited, and when we are in trouble we need to draw on the wisdom of others. None of us can afford either to withdraw into a shell or to be vain and self-opinionated; rather, we need to hear the

opinions of those around us. While it is never easy to distinguish what is valuable and what is not in what we hear, the
ability to do so is a basic element in a secure and prosperous
life.

13. Work and Destiny

If you believe you can conquer anything by force of will, you are sure to slip when you run into unexpected terrain. You must acknowledge forces much greater than personal volition.

When I was twenty-two and working in an electric light company, I came up with a design for a small electrical device that seemed promising. It was not a complex piece of equipment, just a new type of socket, but it let me go into the electrical manufacturing business on my own. While only the most modest of achievements, the decision to produce those sockets was something I had done entirely on my own volition. I chose a path and took it.

Reflecting later on this crossroad in my life, however, I sensed that there was a lot more to it. To be sure, I had made a choice by my own free will, but there were other factors which made that choice possible in the first place. One was the timing. Had I been born twenty or thirty years earlier, I would not have gone into the business of making electrical goods. Then there were my physical condition and family environment. If I had a more robust constitution, if my parents had been alive, and if my brothers had not both passed away in their youth, I'm sure my choices would have been different. That my decision to make electrical appliances was most certainly the result of more than just my own will. The forces of destiny also played a large part.

Whatever historical age they happen to be born into, people manage to create a life for themselves that is in keeping with the times. Conversely, to take up a given occupation one first has to be born into an age appropriate to that occupation. No one could have gone into atomic engineering a century ago, for example. In some respects, then, we act on our own will, but in others we are bound and guided by forces much greater than we are. To be aware of the multiple factors behind a decision can be a source of great strength and inspiration.

If you believe you are acting purely on your own volition, you are bound to come unstuck when things do not go as you planned. If, on the other hand, you know that your actions are profoundly influenced by the broader forces of fate, that awareness helps you acquiesce and gives you reassurance and stability. It is important to make decisions and proceed with your affairs on the basis of your own will and judgment. Still, people's attitudes and opinions vary from one time to another, so it is inevitable that in the course of managing your life, there will be times when you don't know what to do and feel bewildered.

So while your own will is certainly important, it is equally, or probably even more important to temper your will with humble compliance—deference, if you like—that allows you to positively involve yourself in the lot destiny has dealt you. Such an attitude will help you meet life's difficulties without getting flustered, without agonizing over them, and without letting any of them snowball into a threat to your sense of the value of life itself. One important thing that has enabled me to travel the single-minded path of my own career over the past sixty or so years has been just such a sense of destiny that lets me know when to give my will a rest.

14. Enthusiasm and Sincerity

> *Knowledge, wisdom, and ability are all important,*
> *but the most valuable qualities of all are enthusiasm*
> *and sincerity. With these two on your side, anything*
> *can be done.*

I once heard that top insurance salespersons generate as much as a hundred times the revenue in contracts their least successful colleagues can manage. At first I could barely believe it. How could salespeople working for the same company and selling the same insurance achieve such different results? I could think of a few possible reasons: salespeople have different personalities, a factor that affects their ability to sell; and no doubt some know more about insurance, or are just better talkers, than others.

Still, these differences alone couldn't account for such discrepancies in sales. Reflecting on my own experience, I concluded that a more basic factor lay in the degree of enthusiasm and sincerity each member of the sales force brought to the job. An enthusiastic and sincere salesperson is constantly thinking about better ways to approach the customer and always trying out new techniques. When they explain something, such people manage to convey a natural zest even while observing the strictest courtesy. It is difficult, of course, for someone to be enthusiastic and sincere unless they are genuinely convinced that they are doing their customers a service in urging them to buy. When they do show these qualities, however, insurance salespeople are far more likely to win customers. Surely it is this attitude to their daily work that makes some a hundred times more successful than others.

Convinced of the importance of enthusiasm and sincerity, I have always tried to demonstrate a large measure of both. In our company, at least, I don't think anyone has more enthusiasm and sincerity than me as we work together planning and carrying out our activities. Perhaps that is why someone like myself, with little formal education, a feeble body, and no special virtues to speak of, can induce others with far superior talents to work for him and achieve great success. For that reason I firmly believe that the president must always outshine everyone else in the company at least in those two qualities: enthusiasm and sincerity. For it is the president who inspires employees to give their best efforts and brings out the knowledge and skills of each one.

This applies beyond the workplace and apart from executives; for anyone in any area of endeavor, enthusiasm and sincerity are the keys to success. With these two qualities, even someone who cannot speak can find ways to communicate and achieve great things in life. They are infectious, moreover, spreading among colleagues and associates and inspiring them to contribute their best. That, I believe, is how things get done.

15. Learning Is a Tool

Academic learning is strictly a tool. We should be its master, not its slave.

I was raised with little formal education. I left school in the fourth grade, at the age of nine, to take up an apprenticeship in a charcoal brazier shop in Osaka. I didn't do it because I wanted to. I probably wanted to go to school twice as much as most children. How I envied the boy who lived across the street from the store. Every morning as I cleaned out the shop, I would see him come out in his school uniform, and hear his lusty "I'm leaving!" as he left the house. I would have given anything to stay at school, but because of the circumstances in my own home, I could not.

In retrospect, however, being unable to go to school became an advantage in the end. It taught me to respect others and learn from them. As I started up my own business and gradually employed more and more people, I realized that my employees were in one sense superior to me. They had all finished school, and they knew things I did not. I respected them for their education, however, and I was always eager to hear their opinions and suggestions. They responded by fully using their intelligence and talent, each contributing their share to our collective enterprise. Our atmosphere of cooperation and participation has been a major factor in the success of the company.

Naturally, I do not suggest that formal education is unnecessary. Today's world was made possible by our predecessors' dedicated pursuit of learning, and now we need learning even more. But the more necessary formal education becomes, the more careful we must be not to let ourselves be enslaved by it. Once we start believing that we cannot achieve anything without formal learning, we neglect our other resources. Education is a truly splendid thing, but we are not lost, and we can still live productive and rewarding lives without it. It is important to see formal education in a balanced perspective, especially today when more and more people seem to be studying purely for study's sake.

Education and the knowledge it brings are nothing more than tools to help us in our actual lives. Used appropriately, education can be extremely useful, but when abused it can be damaging. In some cases it can harm those whose lives it is supposed to enhance. Knowledge is a tool, and we must learn to use it correctly. Like any tool, those who want to use knowledge optimally must attain the maturity necessary to handle it. Given some of the uses human beings have found for knowledge so far, I can't say we have proven our mastery of it yet.

These days, people are going on to higher and higher levels of education in increasing numbers. It is all the more important not to lose ourselves in the maze of academia, and instead use formal schooling as one means to enrich our lives.

16. Keep on Good Terms with Illness

> *With illness, run the other way and it will come after you. Walk right up to shake its hand, and it will shy away.*

Good health is a priceless asset that cannot be bought, a blessing everyone prays for. Sadly, our prayers are not always answered, and people do become ill. Speaking from experience, let me say this: if you turn away in fear from illness, it will hound you, but if you accept it as part of life, it will leave you alone in the end. Thinking that way is one of the main reasons I have managed to overcome my own poor health and live as long as I have—ninety years, to be precise.

When I was about twenty, I worked for an electric light company. One summer I was returning from a day at the beach and happened to clear my throat. I coughed up phlegm mixed with blood. Immediately I went to see a doctor, who told me I had pulmonary apicitis, or catarrh, and that I should take six months' off and go home to rest. By that time, however, both my parents had passed away, so I didn't really have a home to go to. What is more, in those days I was on a day wage, and we didn't have health insurance plans like we do now. If I took time off from work I'd soon be struggling just to keep myself fed.

I decided it just couldn't be helped. My illness was part of my lot in life, and I would take as much care of myself as I could.

I would work three days, take one off; return to the office for a week, then rest for two days. Oddly enough, though, my condition didn't get any worse. The doctor had warned that I might even die if I didn't take proper care of myself, but the disease didn't develop. I subsequently had a long seesaw battle with the illness, but after the Second World War I grew even healthier than I had been in my youth, and have remained so to this very day.

I am convinced that things turned out this way because I accepted my illness squarely as part of my fate. As such there was no point struggling against it. Instead, I took it as a challenge life had laid down for me, an opportunity to build my character. I greeted my illness head on, willingly made it my companion. That, I'm sure, was one of the key factors contributing to the fortunate outcome of this aspect of my life.

When you think about it, while certainly nothing beats perfect health, falling ill doesn't necessarily have to lead to unhappiness. Sickness has given many people greater insight into life, making them even happier than before, while those who put too much store by their health are often devastated when they lose it. Therefore, the key is not to give in to feelings of self pity and hopelessness upon falling ill, but rather to welcome illness with open arms as a friend who will help you learn and grow. I also believe that this attitude shortens the road to recovery.

My response to illness comes out of personal experience. It might not work for everyone, but I think it is worth considering as one way to deal with disease.

17. Overcoming Anxieties

> *Freedom from cares and worries is the natural state for human beings. Anxieties arise when we look at things from only one narrow perspective.*

Life is full of troubles and anxieties. Sickness, disappointment in love, failure at work—everyone experiences some kind of anguish at one time or another. Anxiety can rob you of sleep or make you irritable and depressed, sometimes to the point of being suicidal. How can worry possibly lead to such tragedy?

It is hard to generalize, for each case has different circumstances, but it seems to me that our troubles swell to overwhelming proportions usually because we get trapped into seeing things from only one perspective. I myself was somewhat of a neurotic. There was something weighing heavily on my mind virtually all the time when I was younger. One of my personal burdens was watching others at work and losing confidence in my own performance, tension building up all the while. I can see clearly now, and I sensed it then, that most of these occasions resulted from my own myopia. Fortunately, I didn't just wallow in my anguish; if I had, I doubt I would still be where I am today. Instead, I tried to distance myself from the mind-set I had formed and overcame the problem by seeing it from another angle.

An example will illustrate what I mean. At one time, when I had about fifty people working for me, a difficult question arose. All of my employees were very hardworking, but there was one who, I discovered, was not completely honest. I didn't want that kind of employee in the company, but I couldn't decide whether or not to fire him. I started losing sleep over it.

As I turned the problem over and over in my mind, a thought occurred to me: I wondered how many wrongdoers there were in all of Japan at that very moment. Assuming, for argument's sake, there were a hundred thousand people in jail, then there must be around five or six times that number whose misdemeanors were unnoticed and unpunished. But it was not as if any of these people had to be sent into exile. Then I thought about the nation, and had to admit that nothing, not even devotion to emperor and country prevented some people from acting in ways that harmed both. (Before World War II, Japanese were encouraged to think of the emperor as semi-divine.) People convicted of serious crimes were of course segregated from society in prisons, but others with minor offenses were pardoned and remained in the community. If that was how the nation dealt with such people, I thought, how could I just fire those I considered to be bad, thereby populating my little realm entirely with virtuous people? Considering the matter in this light, my inner turmoil disappeared, and I decided to be lenient toward the employee in question. My attitude toward my staff grew much more flexible after that.

Countless similar experiences, when everyday problems prodded me into thinking in a new way, turned what seemed like a loss into a gain. Today we are constantly confronting new issues and situations, and it is only to be expected that many things trouble us. Sometimes it seems as if anxiety were the natural human state. We should not be intimidated by or give in to our troubles, for we can do something about them.

Take firm hold of a problem, then turn it around to look at it from as many different angles as possible. You will find that matters which at first glance seem burdensome often turn into productive lessons. This approach offers a way out of specific difficulties, and it can also help you throughout life by dispelling your worry.

It has justified my belief that worry is not our natural state, and that our anxieties are entirely the result of becoming mired in one way of thinking. Broad reflection is the most effective means of conquering the anguish of our hearts.

18. Perseverance

> *Success is a matter of endurance. Keep working away with untiring perseverance, and sooner or later you will succeed.*

There are always times when, despite hard efforts to achieve something, nothing seems to go right, and you feel utterly hopeless. The most important thing is not to lose heart, but to keep your shoulder to the wheel. Things rarely go well right from the start. It takes persistence and unflagging effort before you see any results.

I was twenty-two when I went out on my own to start a small enterprise. I wanted to manufacture a new socket I had designed. It took four months to get to the production stage, and then I could sell barely ten yen's worth—a pittance even in those days. It was hard enough just to buy groceries, let alone continue the business. At that point I might have thrown my hands up and given it all away, and there would have been no Matsushita Electric.

I resolved not to give up. I wanted to keep going, no matter how hard it would be, and not only produce a superior socket, but sell it, too. The end of the year was approaching, bills had to be paid, and I was really in dire straits. Then out of the blue came a request to use my technology to make insulator plates for the base of electric fans. This was the breakthrough that set my business firmly on the path to success.

Many things work out that way. Even when your initial expectations don't materialize, as long as you keep up your efforts, the circumstances around you will change or your vitality and stamina will induce others to help, and unexpected avenues will open up before you.

Once you have made up your mind to do something, don't let slow progress or minor setbacks undermine your determination. Refuse to give in, even when you stumble or your dreams seem ready to shatter. Too many people fail simply because they turned off their path before it could lead them to success. By giving up today, you irrevocably renounce tomorrow's success.

Obsessive perseverance, of course, can become obstinacy. You may be persistent and hardworking, but if you are possessed by some narrow-minded notion and direct your efforts the wrong way, you won't get very far.

Persevere, but move with, not against, the natural course of things. With focus and flexibility, you will be able to carry out your purposes. Success is a matter of endurance. Understand that, and you have one of the secrets of a rewarding life.

19. Self-Assessment

> *It is important to know your own capabilities.*
> *To do that, you must step back and observe*
> *yourself dispassionately.*

One element in a fulfilling life is knowing yourself, having a clear understanding of your own aptitudes and qualities. If you have a firm grasp of who you are, you will be neither conceited nor slavish, but able to give full play to your talents.

Imagine a storekeeper who doesn't have a very good sense of his own strengths and abilities, nor the conviction to act on his own initiative. Instead, he is always watching what others do. So, when his rival next door renovates, he decides he'd better do the same; if the store down the road does a roaring trade by employing a large staff, he decides he should hire more people, too. Our friend is bewildered when the other stores continue to prosper while his languishes. He doesn't understand that he is too easily swayed by what others do, and that makes him launch projects that don't suit his own situation. His passive willingness to look at others without studying himself could eventually cost him his business.

If, on the other hand, he starts out with a secure sense of himself, his business is sure to be a success. Regardless of what his competition does, he may try out something completely new and different, but only if it suits his own unique circumstances. That is the key to his success—knowing his own particular strengths and needs and acting accordingly.

As I noted earlier, however, knowing yourself is not easy. Perhaps you know your inner self better than anyone else possibly could, but in some areas, you might not assess yourself accurately. Many people underestimate their merits, for example, or overrate themselves. Difficult as it may be, however, we need an accurate understanding of ourselves. The question is, how do we arrive at one?

For me, self-observation is the key to self-knowledge. Look at yourself as if from the outside, as if you were observing someone else. That means stepping outside yourself for a moment to take a good look at what you are. Even if you can never actually detach yourself, you can adopt a detached attitude toward yourself, as if you were outside looking on objectively. Self-observation in that sense can help you acquire a more accurate picture of yourself.

An old proverb warns us that "people who go into the mountains lose sight of the mountains." What do you see when you climb Mount Fuji? Just a lot of rocks and gullies. To appreciate the grace and splendor of its overall form, you have to be some distance away. The same is true when you try to see yourself.

Without deliberately setting out to do so, we do, in fact, reflect on ourselves in just this way throughout our daily activities. In the heat of discussion or absorbed in our work, we suddenly become self-conscious and reflect upon what we are doing. What we are doing is viewing ourselves from a distance, reflexively. For most of us, the challenge is to be able to detach ourselves deliberately and productively.

Reflexive self-observation is one way to gain a firmer grasp of who you are. When it becomes easy for you to see yourself dispassionately, you will discover your true potential for success.

20. Everything Has Its Use

The things of this world have value to human beings in some way or other. This idea should be with us all the time as we seek a use for each and every one.

Progress in science and technology has produced a deluge of innovations and goods that people never dreamed possible a short time ago. The sheer volume of new products and conveniences makes it all the more necessary that we be resourceful in learning how to use them wisely; otherwise, we risk wasting or misusing the very achievements that have given us such pride.

Everything in the world—not just human creations—can help or benefit humanity in some way or other. Nothing is useless. There are things around us that may not seem useful now, but someday will be. What we discard today as harmful or unnecessary we will undoubtedly use tomorrow. Throughout history, human beings have never stopped learning more about how to put nature to practical use, and our limitless ingenuity will continue to discover uses for the most unlikely things.

One species of blue mold, for instance, long thought a harmful substance, was found to produce penicillin. Coal and petroleum were once considered no more than black rock and viscous fluid. Besides being sources of energy, they are now used to synthesize chemicals, drugs, plastics, and many other products. All these and more were made possible by the human resourcefulness that fuels progress in science and technology.

It is important to develop the awareness that much of what we now throw away is potentially useful, and make it a policy to discover those uses. This is a mission each of us should accept, but for science and technology, it is their very raison d'être. Unfortunately, not many people think that way. People are not always constructive. They tend to pass over a promising invention even if its strong points far outweigh a single drawback. Rather than trying to correct the one defect, they give up on it.

One of the delicacies Japanese eat during the winter season is globefish (*fugu*), a fish that has deadly poisonous parts such as the ovary and the liver. If our ancestors had shunned the whole fish because of the dreaded poison, they would never have discovered how to enjoy this "most delicious of all fishes." They took up the challenge, studied the location of the poison, and learned how to remove it before cooking. Thanks to their persistent efforts, globefish can be safely eaten. The poison itself is thrown away, but the day may come when it can be used. In fact, research is now going on to find medical uses for globefish poison. If it is successful, globefish will be more than just a gourmet delight.

We have the advantages of advanced science and technology; we ought to be at least as resourceful as our ancestors, who discovered how to make a deadly fish safe to eat, and search aggressively for a use for everything. People can help each other day to day with encouragement, sharing knowledge and ideas. To use what is around us in constructive, beneficial ways is an important task for everyone.

21. Treat Things Well

It pays to understand the inherent characteristics of things and treat them accordingly. Anything that is handled as it should be will respond to human needs.

We have talked about how important it is to understand that virtually everything can be useful, but then we have to think about how to treat things. Above all, we need to know how to use things fully and in the most appropriate fashion. It takes a certain empathy for things, a kind of knack, to make the best use of them.

One person who had this knack was a well-known *shogi* (Japanese chess) professional named Sankichi Sakata (1870–1946). Born in the city of Sakai, Osaka prefecture, in the early Meiji period, he was uneducated, but taught himself shogi and rose to become one of the best players in the country. The Japan Shogi Federation honored him posthumously with coveted titles.

A play was written about Sankichi Sakata called *Osho* [The King]. In one scene the leading character—Sankichi—is well into a game when he realizes that one of his pieces, a silver general, is trapped and unable to maneuver. Under his breath he mutters, "The silver general is weeping." As I will explain, this remark could only come from a great shogi master.

Like chess, shogi is a board game in which each piece is moved one at a time according to fixed rules with the ultimate goal of capturing the opponent's king. A good player knows the strengths and characteristics of each piece and plays them to utilize their capabilities to the full. That ability is what produces great masters of shogi. Sankichi worked hard to bring the potential of every piece into full play in each game. In a sense, he "became" the pieces, which explains how he could project the anguish of being cornered onto the silver general, even though it was only a shogi piece.

With only the most rudimentary knowledge of shogi, I am hardly qualified to comment on Sakata's play, but his empathy for the tools of his trade impressed me, and I believe a similar attitude is necessary in personal life and in business. In my career as an industrialist, I remember a number of occasions when a new experimental item, ready for production, seemed to cry out to me. It needed some change or had some problem. We modified and revised, and in each case, the products that seemed to be appealing to me for help turned out to be really superior after they had been modified.

Every thing that exists has distinctive qualities that can contribute something to our lives. All we need to do is to get an accurate understanding of their nature and potential and handle them accordingly, being careful not to go to extremes in the way we use them. In the spirit of Sankichi Sakata, we would gain a lot if we tried every day to study the things around us and make the best use of them. If we succeed, they will never have to "weep."

22. To Each Season

> *People have different strengths and abilities at different stages in their lives. We should respect those differences among ourselves, expect changes, and make the most of them.*

Starting around the time I turned sixty I began to tire easily and noticed a distinct decline in physical strength. After that I had to face the fact while I might like to carry on as always, I wasn't getting any younger, and that I, like everyone, would change a great deal with the advance of age. Physically, we are at our strongest in our late teens and twenties, passing the peak at around age thirty. In the sport of sumo, which requires concentrated strength stored up for matches that may last only a few seconds, promotion to the highest rank of yokozuna is very unusual after thirty. Even a wrestler strong enough to become a yokozuna in his early twenties finds it almost impossible to maintain the rank ten years later. For all of us, our physical condition starts downhill in the early thirties.

Intellectually, however, our powers continue to grow, peaking at around forty. I am speaking from my own observations, and there are exceptions, but I think others have reached similar conclusions. If, then, physical strength starts declining after thirty and our mental prowess after forty, how is it that people of over forty are able to maintain their positions in society, keep their jobs and carry on in their organizations? How do they manage to work as competently as before? Many, in fact, continue rising to higher posts and show even more outstanding performance on the job. This is partly because in ours and many other countries, society is structured so that older and more experienced people are supported and accorded respect by those who are younger. Their strengths may be different, but they are valued.

Many people in their fifties and sixties are involved in work that requires very sophisticated intellectual powers, and they achieve superior results. A major element in their achievement is the assistance and cooperation of younger people. In terms of physical and intellectual "weight," an older person without that support is at a serious disadvantage compared with someone of thirty or forty.

Unlike the world of sumo, an individual's total strength is not displayed all at once, but this is precisely what makes life so intriguing. It is crucial to be aware of how people change, especially if you are fifty or sixty and in a responsible post like company president. Your performance may be seamless, but you should recognize that it owes a great deal to the cooperation of people in their thirties and forties working under you, guided by your experience and know-how.

Younger people, too, should understand that their abilities are likely to be used more effectively when they take advantage of their seniors' experience. They, too, will age, and so it is important to be willing to learn and amass the experience that will later be needed by their own subordinates.

In sum, abundant experience, keen intellect, and physical stamina are exhibited at different stages in life. We can all strive to take advantage of each other's strengths at each stage in life, whether we are old, young, or in our prime, knowing how human aptitudes change and evolve with age and that cooperation among us can create a more dynamic society.

23. Women and Work

Men and women are different and so are the roles they play in society. Genuine equality recognizes those differences and allows men and women to perform optimally in their appropriate roles.

Women have recently begun to take jobs outside the home in such numbers that they are becoming a significant part of the work force. This development is good for the economy and for society. My only reservation lies in what seems to me a too literal interpretation of "equality" between men and women. It is impossible for men and women to be the same in everything, in every way. Individuals are unique, each with inherent traits and abilities distinct from anyone else. People are equal in that they are human, and therefore equally endowed with individual characteristics, not because they all possess the same characteristics. Equality of women and men does not mean that the two are the same, or that men and women should act or think in the same way. It means, I believe, the freedom of both men and women to perform to their full potential in accordance with their respective aptitudes and chosen roles.

Some characteristics and roles of men and women are inherent to their gender. Some traits emerge in the way people live. Although there are exceptions, neither men nor women were meant to live out their lives alone. Some decide for one reason or other to remain single throughout their lives, but as a general rule human beings form couples, which is considered the usual, natural pattern of behavior for the human species.

This arrangement creates a natural division of labor, between the wife, who is biologically equipped for childbirth and feeding of infants, and the husband, who is not. In our society, as a norm, the man goes out to work and the woman takes care of the family and runs the household. This creates a complementary relationship, nurturing a healthy family that supports the society as a whole.

While this may be the normative and natural pattern, in Japan there has been an unfortunate added dimension. Sometimes called male chauvinism, it is a value judgment that relegates the female sex to a position inferior to the male and casts her role within the home as less important than the man's work outside. This pervasive view, once the rule throughout Japan, seriously distorts the relative value of roles. Neither work outside the home or that within the home should be given higher or lower priority. Both are equally important.

Nowadays men and women are increasingly assigning themselves identical roles. This may be a good idea in theory, but in actual life, it is extremely difficult to put into practice. It is asking too much, for example, to expect a woman who bears and raises children, to perform outside the home the same as a man, at least during the time when her children are still very young. It seems more reasonable for both sexes to take up different roles at different times, according to their biological functions, and natural talents and inclinations. Such a flexible approach would give both equal weight and importance. In this basic frame of reference, we could achieve real contentment, a man and woman each finding fulfillment in his or her respective role.

Dividing up roles "naturally," moreover, should not be interpreted to mean that women should not take jobs outside the household. The advance of women into the work force is a positive, and in many ways natural, development. Technological progress and the diversification of lifestyles have created many occupations that are well-suited to—in fact, require—the special talents of women. Putting the right woman in the right job makes the best use of her particular capabilities and helps society as well. Even if a woman leaves her salaried job upon marriage or childbirth, that experience helps her immeasurably in dealing with the realities of society outside the family that will stand her in good stead, whatever role she might play.

I sincerely support the movement of women into more visible positions in society and their efforts to pursue lifelong careers, but I believe this trend will backfire if people do not fully appreciate the value of the inherent role of women to have children, and consequently, become the mainstay and guardian of the household at least during the years of child-rearing. Our society as a whole needs to recognize and value that role more than it does at present. The advance of women into the work force will only succeed if it is premised on a full understanding of the role they have played in the household, whether her role was molded by history or biology. When that understanding is achieved, I think we can hope for true equality between men and women.

24. Responsibility of Parents

> *Parents should have a solid, coherent philosophy of life. If they live and work in accordance with that philosophy, they will earn the respect of their children.*

As the saying goes, "It is easy to become a parent, but quite another thing to be a parent." The hardest thing about parenthood is the longest and largest part—training and education of children.

Our literature and speech are filled with aphorisms like "the character formed at age three survives to 100," and "strike while the iron is hot," reminding us that children must be trained and taught in the behavior and traditions of their society from early childhood to adulthood. People cannot find their way through life without this guidance. The infant girl raised with wolves in the Indian wilderness discovered decades ago could only howl like a wolf and could not be rehabilitated into human society. No matter how intelligent, a person needs to be given direction and training while still young.

Providing this guidance for children is the role and responsibility, in the broad sense, of adult society as a whole. But it is the parents who hold the greatest responsibility through their close and daily interchange with the child. Inasmuch as they have given birth to children, they are responsible for their training and education, and it can be a most difficult endeavor.

Various methods have been tried. In preindustrial Japan, for example, the children of merchant families were often placed with the proprietors of other shops to receive training as apprentices.

I am the parent of one child, but because I was so preoccupied with the affairs of my business, I ended up leaving his education and training entirely to my wife. I may not be qualified to speak about the discipline and training of children, therefore, but there is one principle that I believe is of paramount importance: A parent should have a firm philosophy of life and view of society.

A parent should always teach and discipline a child directly, indicating clearly what is allowed, what is not, and what must be done. It is perhaps even more important, however, for a parent to believe and act in accordance with a specific view of life and society. This view forms the basis of convictions that are unconsciously and imperceptibly manifested in word and deed, and transmitted thereby to one's offspring. If parents have no such convictions or views, any instruction or advice they might give will have little, if any, value or persuasiveness.

If you have become a parent, you have to seek or create some kind of coherent philosophy on life and society. This goes for both father and mother, but in one respect perhaps fathers need to be more deliberate in forming that philosophy. In our modern society, there are many fathers, myself included, who have few opportunities for closeness with their children. But if a father has a firm set of general principles, they will probably be reflected in the thinking of the mother and passed on to the children. If the father has no principles worth passing on, on the other hand, and the mother has none of her own, the children's upbringing may be dominated by emotion and affection without the conceptual base that is needed for the proper guidance of growing children.

Many problems parents struggle with today, it seems to me, stem from their own lack of firm principles and convictions. This poverty of philosophy is one element behind the undesirable behavior we see among some young people. The considerable diversification of values that is occurring now, in our post-industrial society, may make it more difficult to establish a well-formed outlook on life, and yet we must, building on our own daily experience and convictions. This is only the starting point in fulfilling our responsibility to train and educate our children, but it can also be our point of departure as we chart better paths for our own lives as well.

25. Live Life to the Full

Now is only a brief moment. But don't let it slip by.
If we live each moment to the full, the accumulated
hours and days will brim with the vigor of youth.

When I was about seventy-five years old, I had the pleasure of meeting the distinguished wood sculptor Denchu Hiragushi, who was then close to the age of one hundred. His career spanned the three tumultuous eras of modern Japanese history—Meiji (1868–1912) during which Japan transformed itself into a modern state, Taisho (1912–26) when democracy and liberal ideas flourished, and Showa (1926–89) which saw militarization, war, defeat, reconstruction and rapid economic growth. Hiragushi was among the most accomplished sculptors of his times. Our encounter was made memorable by his remark, "At age sixty or seventy, Mr. Matsushita, you are a mere urchin! Let me tell you, the prime of a man's life begins after one hundred. I'm just getting started!"

By any ordinary standard, both of us were well advanced in age, long eligible for retirement, but his youthfulness of spirit filled me with amazement and admiration. Afterward I learned that one of Hiragushi's pet phrases was, "If you don't do it now, when will you?" And another, "If I don't do it myself, who will?"

When Hiragushi celebrated his one-hundredth birthday somewhat later, I learned that seasoning in his garden he had enough wood to last another fifty years. He had already impressed me at our first meeting with his irrepressible vitality, but now, considering all that wood, I knew he must have been serious when he said "the prime of a man's life begins at one hundred!" It was even more incredible to think of the tenacity and devotion of a wood sculptor who apparently believed that it would take another fifty years to perfect his craft.

Hiragushi carried on his work well after he reached one hundred. At one point he contributed an essay to the monthly magazine, *PHP.* He wrote:

> If I don't live a little longer, I cannot fulfill my responsibility to a number of works that remain. I must complete five or six, at the very least four of them. Recently, I finished one, apart from those four, but it was extremely difficult; it took three years of toil and struggle, and it was very hard on me. I finally concluded that all my years of training had been a farce. For five or ten years after beginning to study this art, a novice should do nothing but carve subjects faithfully in wood. I didn't get that kind of training. I simply got by through sheer cleverness.

This passage affected me deeply and became an inspiration and encouragement in my endeavors after that time. Here was a man twenty-two years my senior, not only absorbed in his work and bursting with energy and enthusiasm, but also able to criticize his own training and still working hard to do better, even though he was at the very pinnacle of his profession. The essay fairly trembled with his seriousness of purpose.

Mr. Hiragushi passed away on October 2, 1979, just before his 108th birthday. He did not use up the fifty-year stock of wood, but considering his unflagging dedication and attachment to his work until the very end, I think he lived the life he wanted to live, from start to finish. His eternal youthfulness of spirit must have come from his ability to live from moment to moment in the conviction that if he didn't do something right away, he might not be able to do it at all, and that if he didn't do it himself, perhaps no one would.

None of us knows when our life will come to an end, but we all hope we can live each moment to do the things we ought to do, until the last minute. But few of us, regardless of our sincerity, can actually live so intensely. Still, it is possible, and the vitality and verve of a man like Hiragushi are an inspiration.

26. In Search of Fulfillment

Our work holds a very important place in the fabric of our lives; if we can find meaning in our work, we will have found the keys to happiness in living.

Inasmuch as we have been given the gift of life, we all want to feel that our presence in the world is important, that our life is worth living. There is no satisfaction or contentment simply in coasting aimlessly along from one day to the next. People seek meaning in life in any number of ways: through hobbies and sports, homemaking, or watching the children grow. Some feel their life is at its best when they are squirreling away money or dining on fine food. That which makes living meaningful is different for each of us, and that is the way it should be.

If asked what has given the most meaning to my own life, I would say that it changed several times. After entering an apprenticeship in Osaka at the age of nine, I often cried into my pillow at night out of homesickness for my home and my mother, but as I became accustomed to the work of the bicycle shop, I began to dream of rising at least to senior employee and having five or six apprentices under my direction. I threw myself into my work from early morning to late at night, completely forgetting the passage of time.

The 1900s was not a time when we thought much about the kind of work that would have meaning for our lives; I was still very young and not concerned about such things. Yet in retrospect, I did work with a sense of purpose and savored the satisfaction of knowing when a job was well done. From that point of view, I did sense what we call "meaning in life."

When I was fifteen, I took a job with an electric company and worked as a wiring technician. I did my best to improve my skills and do good work, and I was eager to be treated with respect by my co-workers and superiors. I helped with a number of difficult and challenging projects, often working many hours overtime and sometimes staying up all night to meet a deadline. I always had a tremendous feeling of accomplishment when a job was completed successfully.

At the age of twenty-two, my life took another turn when I left the electric company and started my tiny workshop manufacturing electric wiring fixtures. At first I was so absorbed with getting the business off the ground that I had no time to think about intangible rewards. We simply worked as hard as we could. But I remember how, after finishing up work late on a midsummer's night, I would soak in the tub, glad that I had put in a good day's work and give myself a pat on the back. What I was doing gave me fulfillment and direction in life. As the company became much larger, I continued to enjoy a full life. We made it a company mission to contribute to the culture and growth of society, very large goals that brought all the members of the corporation together in a common cause that was eminently rewarding.

So, as in my own case, the occupation or goal that offers the greatest fulfillment does not necessarily remain the same, but changes with the events of one's life. For me, the changes were healthy and timely. Some people, such as followers of religion and artists, maintain the same pursuit throughout their lives, and I have great admiration for their dedication. The majority, however, cannot afford the luxury of single-minded commitment. They derive ultimate meaning in life from the completion of one endeavor at a time. When one goal has been achieved, they move on to the next. The value of the endeavor is the same, regardless of the duration.

Work can be a rich source of meaning in life. It occupies a very important position in our lives, both economically and in terms of time. Even though many activities are deeply rewarding, work ought at least to be among them, if not the major one. It can make the difference between happiness and discontent.

It is important to be able to enjoy hobbies, to spend time with and enjoy one's family and experience variety in one's life, but I believe that the satisfaction from all one's other activities hinges basically on whether we devote ourselves to our work and find enjoyment and satisfaction in it. Work is not everything, but it should be among the pursuits from which one feels the greatest reward.

27. Toward Better Lives

> *A constant pattern of production and consumption forms a rhythm in our lives. Since it is so pervasive, our lives will be much more fulfilling if we try, physically and spiritually, to achieve better production and more optimal consumption.*

Life is precious. It is a journey each individual travels alone over a path that cannot be retraced. Most of us fervently hope, therefore, that our lives will have meaning and purpose. First, we need to know what life is and to form for ourselves a working definition, in order to conceptualize its meaning for us. The more thoroughly we understand life, the better we can make it.

After launching the "Peace and Happiness through Prosperity" movement in 1946, I studied the question, "What is life?" at considerable length. Most people think of life as the span of years between birth and death. On another level, however, it is the accumulation of the deeds and thoughts of each day, each hour. A close look at our daily routine tells a lot about the nature of life. After a great deal of thought, I came to the conclusion that basically human life is a constant replay of production and consumption.

We usually think of production and consumption in economic terms, but they can serve as useful concepts to describe other aspects of our physical and spiritual lives as well. In daily life, they are basic. Every day we produce things, tangible and intangible, on the one hand, and we consume things on the other. With each process we exercise our minds in one way or other. In production, you visualize the item or endeavor and proceed to develop and devise ways to make it real. Consumption of goods or services or ideas, also involves mental effort. A consumer makes choices, assesses and enjoys the quality of the product or service.

We can lead more meaningful and constructive lives through the pursuit of activities that will assure a better today than yesterday, a better tomorrow than today. Politicians work to do more for their constituents, educators try to improve their teaching skills. People in all occupations aim for improvement. The efforts of all, added together, assure the positive development of society as a whole and happier, more fulfilled lives for each individual.

It may be easier to think of life in terms of production and consumption rather than "the meaning of life" or "purpose in life." Although in this sense they are the same, learning how to do better at both paves the way to a happier life and brings the question "What is life?" into more immediate focus. I have found that stopping from time to time to consider what I could do to enhance my own production and consumption was helpful in renewing a sense of fulfillment in my life.

28. Your Time on Earth

Live with courage, hope and conviction,
making the fullest possible use of the time heaven
has given you.

I never expected to live a long life. I was frail to begin with, and from about the age of twenty, while working for the Osaka Electric Light Company, I suffered from bouts with pulmonary catarrh. For many years after I started my own business I had to have frequent medical care. During the war, when we were all pressed to work at a frenzied pace, I began to spend less time in bed and gradually found myself in surprisingly fine fettle. Over the years that followed, I was healthy and continued to be active, even at ninety. I believe that my health and long life are the work of destiny, and I can only be profoundly grateful.

When I was around fifty-five or fifty-six, not long after the end of World War II, I went to see a fortune-teller. The initial turmoil following the ceasefire had abated, but the country still suffered from shortages and poverty. Because of the Occupation purge of wartime industry, restrictions had been hastily and mistakenly slapped on the company and I couldn't proceed with the rebuilding of my business. It took some time to get the designation of Matsushita Electric as a zaibatsu rescinded, and in the meantime my assets were frozen and my activities restricted. I agonized over the future. Encouraged by a friend, and figuring there was nothing to be lost in learning what insights a fortune-teller might have to offer, I actually visited three in succession.

The first of the three announced instantly upon examining my palms that I would live a very long life. The second said the same thing in a different way: "You will not die before you are seventy or eighty." And the third declared that he had never seen palms like mine and that I would definitely live a long time. It was very reassuring to have three palmists deliver the same verdict.

I was much healthier at the time than I had been in my younger days, but their pronouncements nonetheless came as a total surprise. I was actually more dismayed than elated. I thought I knew my own constitution, and I was inclined to be skeptical about such a happy prediction. But the two or three friends who made the rounds with me all received readings indicating shorter lifespans. The fortune-tellers even showed me the differences on my palms to prove their accuracy. Today, all of the friends that accompanied me that day have passed away and here I am. I never believed in the art of palmistry, but after the death of my friends, it became harder to dismiss its prophecies.

I have been fortunate to enjoy a long life and am grateful for this destiny, but basically, only heaven knows the length of a person's lifespan. How long one will live is probably forever unknown, but that does not mean our lifespan is totally under the control of forces beyond us. Our own power and effort have a great deal to do with how long we live.

As I mentioned earlier, I believe that ten or twenty percent of our life depends on the efforts of the individual. I suggested that we should consider this margin of human intervention, our chance to add that extra shine to our destinies. The same may be said for our lifespan. If heaven determines ninety percent, the remaining ten percent is up to each of us. We are responsible to a certain extent for how long we live.

What is the "natural" lifespan of human beings? On a trip to China I was told by several people that in China it is thought to be 160 years, and 80 years is called "half a life." Scientific studies suggest that if all the various hazards of life were removed, the actual lifespan of humans could be between 150 and 200 years. In Japan, which has the highest longevity rate in the world, the record lifetime is 124 years.

Therefore, if I continue taking care of myself and count my blessings, there is every reason to believe that I will live quite a bit longer from this writing. When I turned ninety by the old way of age reckoning in Japan (a person is one year old at birth), I made up my mind to try for a shot at a new record, say 130. Even failing that, however, the important thing is to have a goal and set your sights on it, living each day with that goal in mind. How close you can get to your target you will never know; the least you can do with the life and health you are fortunate enough to enjoy is to carry on as best you can as long as you can with courage and hope. At least that is what I have made my policy and guide.